Home SWEET ORGANIZED HOME

Inspiring | Educating | Creating | Entertaining

Brimming with creative inspiration, how-to projects, and useful information to enrich your everyday life, quarto.com is a favorite destination for those pursuing their interests and passions.

Better Homes & Gardens.

© 2022 by Quarto Publishing Group USA Inc.
Text © 2022 by Jessica Litman

Photography © Jessie Hearn Photography
Pages 6, 7, 9, 12, 14, 27, 42, 64, 66, 71, 76, 82, 87, 94, 95, 106, 125, 129, 160

Photography © Jessica Litman
Pages 13, 29, 35, 40, 51, 61, 73, 102, 109

All other photography © Shutterstock

First published in 2022 by Rock Point, an imprint of The Quarto Group,
142 West 36th Street, 4th Floor, New York, NY 10018, USA
T (212) 779-4972 F (212) 779-6058 www.Quarto.com

Rock Point titles are also available at discount for retail, wholesale, promotional, and bulk purchase. For details, contact the Special Sales Manager by email at specialsales@quarto.com or by mail at The Quarto Group, Attn: Special Sales Manager, 100 Cummings Center Suite 265D, Beverly, MA 01915 USA.

10 9 8 7 6 5 4 3 2 1

ISBN: 978-1-63106-823-2

Library of Congress Control Number: 2021946242

Publisher: Rage Kindelsperger
Creative Director: Laura Drew
Senior Managing Editor: Cara Donaldson
Editor: Keyla Pizarro-Hernández
Cover and Interior Design: Evelin Kasikov

Printed in China

Home
SWEET
ORGANIZED
HOME

DECLUTTER & ORGANIZE YOUR BUSY FAMILY

Jessica Litman
the organized mama

ROCK
POINT

CONTENTS

Introduction

I have seen so many people transform their outlook on life simply by organizing their homes. I know it sounds silly. You're probably thinking, "How can I transform my outlook on life with organizing? It doesn't seem logical." But when you understand what organizing does, you can see how transformative and life-changing it can be.

My goal in writing this book on organizing is to show you how you can change your habits to lead an organized life. When you have order in your home, you create order in your life and are able to deal with things that are outside of your control. When you are struggling with life, the order that can be found in organizing is so refreshing. You can simply sit back and appreciate the order you created, even when everything else around you is falling apart.

When you start living with things in order, you end up focusing on other things that really inspire or interest you. You stop focusing on what isn't working. You stop looking at things with a glass-half-empty perspective and begin looking at things from a glass-half-full perspective, which I believe is a much better outlook on life.

Growing up, I was always an organized person. I always made my bed and lined up my dolls and stuffies in a row on my bed each night. My school desk was always tidy. I never had chores because I always kept my room clean. My parents never had to worry about my organizing habits because I had them from birth. My dad is like that and so was his mom. This crazy organizing ability might be genetic.

I discovered that organizing was going to be my lifeline early in life. I experienced some traumatic life events at a very young age. And with those life events, organizing helped me feel in control in uncertain times. I wasn't sure about much, but I knew that when I went to my bedroom, things were organized. I felt calm. I could simply just be. If I didn't have a space that was organized, I am not sure I would be who I am today. That is why I am so passionate about teaching families how to organize and create habits that support order. When you have order, your brain just works better.

As a former teacher, I always thought that brain research was so interesting because it showcased how kids learn and understand information. There is so much information out there on how the brain processes things. My favorite brain-related topic is how organizing and order benefit brain function and brain development in children.

When I decided to retire my teaching hat, the teacher in me never really went away. I think that is true with anyone who was or is a teacher—it never really leaves you. The teacher in me helped me teach families how to organize their homes, and that is what I have done for the past eight years through my business, The Organized Mama.

As The Organized Mama, I have made it my mission to help families tackle order in their homes. Because when things are organized, you just feel better.

And no one has time for disorganization when there are kiddos running around, am I right?!

So, if you're a parent who is looking to create lasting organization at home or you're looking to creating lasting organizing habits, you've come to the right place! In this book, I break down everything I have learned from both teaching and organizing so I can share it with you. You will learn how to tweak and change your habits to create the order you want so you can spend more time on things you love doing instead of searching for your things.

Throughout this book, I share different ways that you can organize different rooms in your home in a specific order that helps you stay organized. The room chapters are in the order I feel is best to tidy up your home based on my experience as a professional organizer. In the following chapters, you'll also learn various organizing habits that can be used to keep those spaces organized after all your hard work getting them tidy. Some habits can be used interchangeably while others may only apply to one space. Pick habits you know you can stick with because when you make those changes, you can keep your home organized for good!

I also share lists for how you can create long-lasting organizing habits for yourself and your family and keep track of your progress. These are suggestions because not everyone's definition of organized is going to be the same. I am rather realistic when it comes to organizing. Not everything needs to be in matching bins. Not everything needs to be color-coded. If you like that, then do it. If not, then don't. But you need to start creating habits that will help you and your family get organized. You have to find things that you will actually stick with instead of just trying to do "what the cool kids are doing."

And lastly, at the end of this book, you will find worksheets to help you get organized as you go. The worksheets are there to help you get started, but use them as you feel is needed. I teach my clients how to change small things that make a big impact on maintaining order in their homes. Start small and find areas you can change to create order for the organized home you envision. But be realistic with yourself and your family. Pick the things that you think will work for you. Find things that will support your family in your mission to get organized. These habits will help everyone in your family find order.

With all my years of teaching, I've learned that you need to break down what to expect for different age groups of kids and what they should and can be doing in terms of organizing. This will help you teach them organizing habits that will benefit them throughout their lives.

I hope to instill in you organizing habits that will help your family maintain order. I have real-life stories of clients I have worked with, so you know this isn't just something my family does. It is something that anyone can do. I also want you to be able to do it. I want you to be able to organize and keep those habits, so your home is orderly and you can feel more in control of your life.

Let's get started.

CHAPTER 1

What Does Being "Organized" Mean to You?

I have a story for you. Back when I first started organizing, I had a client who wanted help with her daughter's bedroom. She told me she couldn't keep it organized because of all the stuff her daughter had in her room. She wanted a plan for all the toys and clothes and desk supplies. So, I created a plan for her daughter's bedroom and got rid of the junk. Gave everything a specific spot for stuff to go. Like all her doll clothes went into a drawer in her closet, and the accessories fit under her bed.

Less than a week later, that same client called saying that her daughter's bedroom wasn't organized. So, I asked some questions to follow up. What wasn't organized? What was bothering her? What wasn't working? I quickly found out that she didn't like all the stuff in her daughter's room. Which meant that she wanted that stuff to be stored in a different location. I missed the cardinal rule of organizing: getting really clear on what "organized" means to that client.

After that experience, I learned to always get a clear definition for what "organized" means, which is why we have to start this book with the chapter on defining what organizing means to you. What does being organized look like for you and your family?

Now a quick note: There are many different words for *organized,* such as *orderly, tidy*, and *clutter-free*. All of these words mean the same thing. So if you see them on social media or in an article, just know they all mean *organized*.

If you don't have a clear understanding of what organized means within the four walls of your home, then you will never feel like you have it in your home. You have to get super clear on what this word means for you and your family to truly *feel* like you have an organized home. Because once you get crystal clear on that, you can easily get yourself organized, no matter how you define it. And maybe, just maybe, you already have order in your home, and you don't even know it because you haven't clearly defined it for yourself yet.

Let's start at the very beginning. (I hope you sang that like Julie Andrews in *The Sound of Music*!) If you are sitting or standing somewhere in your house, I want you to do a quick exercise with me and take a look around. Stop reading for a second and scan the room you are sitting or standing in right now (if you're not at home at the moment, you can do this later). After doing a quick scan around the room, what thoughts popped into your head? Were you focusing on the toys that needed to be put away? Or the pile of dishes near the sink? Or the storage boxes in the corner? Or how you really want to repaint the walls in the room? Fill out the worksheet on page 135 to answer these questions.

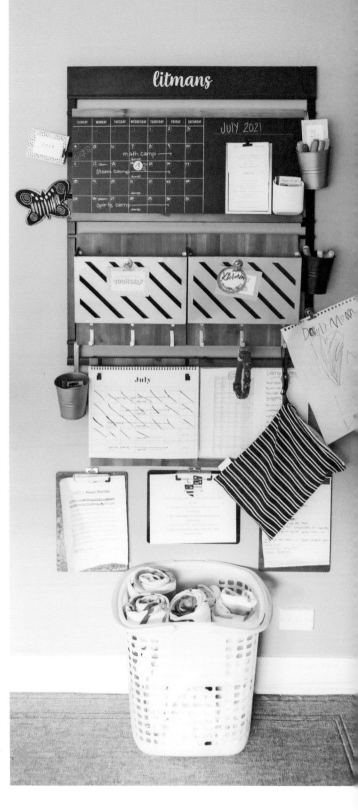

Okay, now I want you to look around the room again, and this time find the spaces or areas that you feel are organized, tidy, or orderly. Then answer these questions:

- Why did you feel like that space was organized?

- What emotions did you feel when you looked at that space?

It is really easy to decide that something is disorganized, but focusing on what is organized changes your whole perspective. You are able to figure out what exactly organized looks like to you. Then you can recreate that orderly feeling in every room of your home without having to look on social media to get inspired!

Now that you already found one area of your home that you deem to be orderly, all you have to do is find a few more tidy spaces. This will give you a visual reminder that your home is organized! It is easy for us to forget that sometimes, especially us parents. You are an organized person; you just have a different way of organizing because you have kids. Seriously, it is a fact, and you can't change that!

Not every area is completely picture-worthy, but I still like the pretty aesthetic that order brings to my home. But this isn't always the case for most homes I go into to help organize. This is why finding what organized means to you is how you are going to live a calmer and more orderly life!

FINDING YOUR ORGANIZED HOME

Now that you have identified all the organized areas of your home, use the five-step guide on page 11 to help define what an organized home means to you. This is how you are going to go forward to determine whether your home is orderly. Only you can say what organized looks like for you in your home. I want you to really get comfortable with that idea so you can make organizing easier for yourself.

What to do if you can't find anything organized in your home? If that's the case, try to organize one drawer exactly how you envision it in your head. Maybe you want to keep only a few items in that drawer; if so, move everything else to a different drawer. Try to keep that one drawer organized to your liking.

Look at that drawer. Write down the emotion you feel when you open that drawer. Then write why you like the drawer organized that way. Use that newly organized drawer as your standard for how you want your entire home to be. But don't worry. You don't have to do this alone! I have more helpful tips in the rest of this book.

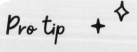

Pro tip

If you can't find anything that is organized in your home and the idea of organizing a drawer feels a little overwhelming right now, then try to find other areas of your life that are organized and use that as your guide!

FIVE STEPS TO ORGANIZING YOUR HOME

1. Start with the first room you feel is organized. Go back to that space and look at the area.

2. Write down why you feel that space is organized. Is it because everything has a designated space where it goes? Is it because you only have a few things hanging in that closet? Is it because everything in that space isn't touched by anyone other than you?

3. Now write down the emotion you feel when you look at that space. I want you to focus on the emotion because it is also part of the definition of what being organized means to you.

4. Repeat for each room in your home.

5. Once you go through each room, ask yourself why you want to become more organized. Is it because you feel obligated or because you know it will be life-changing, stress-reducing, and just all-around better for your mental well-being? Getting to the why of organizing will help you on your journey. When you know why you want something, it can help you execute your plans in a more efficient manner. As parents, we don't have a lot of spare time to just sit and recreate stuff from the Internet. So, let's take a hot minute to determine whether it makes sense for our homes to look Pinterest-worthy, or whether we are fine with our own definition of orderly. This last step is now your new definition of organized. You are on your way to an organized home that is just right for you!

WHAT DOES BEING ORGANIZED HAVE TO DO WITH HABITS?

I could ramble on for pages about habits you should be doing in your home to stay organized, but if that is not your end game, then what is the point? Defining what organizing means to you will help you make organization a habit and keep your home tidy. A habit is anything you do over and over again, such as emptying the dishwasher every morning or mindlessly scrolling social media.

When we look at organizing, we have to look at our habits around organizing. These are things we do in order to keep our home tidy or leave it a cluttered mess.

Pro tip

Create a simple habit tracker to help you keep tabs on the habits that may or may not be working for you and your family.

I am not here to judge what organizing means to you because your home is not my home and what works for me may not work for you. And vice versa. But when you set habits for yourself, you will be organizing your home for you, not for anyone else. And that is going to be life-changing. You won't read this and do everything I say. You'll read this and decide what you want to change and what you can live with. You'll figure out with your family what is important to you and what doesn't matter. You can look at organized home pictures online and decide whether that is the home you want to live in or whether your home is perfect just the way it is.

I do not believe that organizing is a one-size-fits-all type of thing. Each family works in its own way. Some people may define organized as everything in perfect rows; others may define it as being tidy-ish. Organized-ish. Orderly-ish.

So, when you look at your habits, ask yourself whether or not they are working for you to have an orderly home. Use the list on the next page to help you.

DECLUTTERING

In the world of organization, decluttering is an important habit in keeping things tidy and maintaining lasting order. If your goal is to keep a tidy home, then decluttering is a must. Decluttering is the act of removing clutter or unnecessary items from your house. That could mean donating, selling, throwing away, or recycling items.

Clutter can often take up a whole space or overcrowd a space and prevent you from keeping your home as organized as you would like. For most families, clutter can happen when items are left out on counters and things begin to pile up and the piles of items get bigger. Then someone needs an item and the entire house is torn apart to find it.

Pro tip

Research local donation centers where you can donate some of your things.

Instead of letting things pile up, put an item away when you see it out. The faster you do this, the less things will pile up and the easier it will be to maintain your organizing habits. If you aren't sure where an item should go or whether you even use it, then think about decluttering that item.

As you start creating organizing habits that will work for you and your family, start to also think about ways to keep your spaces clutter-free.

Organize Like a Pro

Use this simple list to get started on keeping track of your organizing habits. Check out the worksheets on pages 136 and 137 to answer more specific questions about your current habits.

- List your current habits.
- Write a list of habits you'd like to start doing and a list of habits you'd like to change.
- Grab a piece of paper, poster board, or whiteboard and create a table with various columns for the days of the week.
- Write down which habits you'd like to do each day.
- Use the tracker to help you stay consistent and check off what you actually did each day.
- Make tweaks as needed.

CHAPTER 2

Creating Lasting Organizing Habits

Some of your current habits may not be working for you or your family. That just means that particular habits need some tweaking, not your entire home! I have seen too many people believe that they have no order in their homes when they just need a few spaces tweaked. Remember, you're just adjusting a few habits specific to you and your family's needs to create lasting organizing habits.

Have you ever gotten a new planner, thinking that it will keep you on track, but after about a week you stop using it because you never carry the planner with you, so you never write things in it? The planner isn't the problem; it's your habits around the planner that are not working for you. Same goes with organizing. Bins and products aren't going to fix a habit that isn't working. You have to start by changing or tweaking what you are actually doing.

HOW TO TWEAK AN ORGANIZING HABIT

As you begin creating habits and ask yourself the necessary questions (see the worksheets on pages 138 to 140), think about which habits you need to tweak.

Let's say you feel that your closet organizing habits are not working for you. You notice that in the morning you never put your pajamas away because they end up on the floor of your closet rather than the dresser drawer in your room. And at the end of the day, you never hang up your work pants because you don't have enough space for them. How can you find more space in your closet to make sure your pants and pajamas are easy to put away? You start by looking at other areas of your closet and bedroom. You notice that inside your dresser drawers, you have plenty of space for your T-shirts and athleisure wear. This means that those items can move out of your closet and into your dresser drawer. In this scenario, the habit that needs tweaking is the location of your items, not your entire closet.

Pro Tip

If it gets too overwhelming, do one small thing each week.

Let's say you start by grouping your items together based on how you wear them, not by color. So, all your work clothes, including pants, are hung together. This will help you create a habit for finding specific clothes. Then you move the drawer where your pajamas go to your closet so you can put them away every morning. By rearranging items in your closet, you create more room for your pants and a spot for your pajamas. By looking at how you are using the space and tweaking where items go, you make it easier to keep the room tidy.

Simple shifts in our organizing habits will lead to order because we are tweaking, not changing everything. When you break down which habits aren't working, you aren't wasting time and energy on things that are! This will help you create habits throughout your home that will work and endure.

When I first started going into people's homes to organize, I offered a weekly tidying service. This service was where I would tidy up a small space in someone's home, then the following week I would change a different area that we would agree upon prior to my visit. These small changes lasted because we weren't changing everything at once. We changed small things that the family could handle each week. So, tweaking your habits slowly but consistently works to create lasting change in your home! When you are living with lots of people, you have to create organizational systems that work for everyone, not just one person.

HABIT TWEAKING GUIDE

Ready to start tweaking some habits? Pick one habit at a time when going through this list. Follow it in order and go through this list for each habit you want to tweak.

- Pick one organizing habit to tweak.
- Decide what is not working in that area.
- Make a plan to change a small thing in that area.
- Continue tweaking until you feel it meets your definition of organized.

 MAINTAINING ORDER

As I mentioned earlier, to start changing your organizing habits, you first have to identify what you don't like and what you want to change. Then you can start thinking of things you want to do instead. This is crucial for maintaining what you envision for your home. This is *your* gold standard for keeping things tidy. Next, set up habits to meet that standard. Once you have your clear vision of what organizing will look like in your home, then you can create systems to keep things organized. That is where you change your habit.

The number one reason people feel they can't get organized is because of other family members or roommates. Believe me, I totally have been there! I have heard that exact sentiment countless times from clients and people on social media. Typically, you have at least one disorganized person in your household. The struggle to keep your home organized is hard.

What I often see is people changing all their organizing habits to create order. The problem with that way of thinking is that the least organized person in the house is not going to follow those new habits. Their old habits will probably stay in place unless the new habits are things they are willingly to adopt.

So how do you go about maintaining order when that one (or two or three) individual won't follow any of the organization habits you just created? You start organizing your entire home for the least organized person.

Why would you want to organize for the most disorganized person in your household? Because that is the person who will struggle to keep up with your organizing habits. You are organized and can maintain order in many different ways, but the disorganized person cannot. So, by creating a system that works for that person, you are now setting them up to meet your idea of organization.

 MANAGING EXPECTATIONS

We really have to manage our expectations when we are creating organizing habits. Yes, it can be so relaxing watching people fill up empty canisters with food and laundry items. But is that something you are going to keep up with? Can you do it more consistently, or is it a task that will end up taking up space because you will just use the containers the item comes in?

You also have to manage the expectations of what your family can do. What are you willing to accept from them? What can you let go of? What do you need to do to keep order in your home? Getting really clear on your expectations will help you get

a better idea of what you need and want the entire family to do. Do not overthink this, but do be honest with yourself.

We all have different organizing habits, so you might have an organizing habit that only works for you and others may not find it helpful. Or your loved ones may not do it at all. You have to be okay with that if you find your definition of organizing is different from your family's. I know mine is and I am okay with that. I have my set expectations for what they have to do and what I will do to organize behind them as they go.

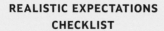

REALISTIC EXPECTATIONS CHECKLIST

Ask yourself the following questions to figure out whether what you expect your family to do is realistic or will just make you upset. You want to be very clear about what's possible and what would really work for your family.

- What do you want your home to look like?

- Are your expectations realistic?

- Can all your family members do this independently?

- What do you need to put in place to make sure your family member(s) can do this task?

- Have you given detailed instructions for how you want this to go?

- Have you tested this out to see whether your family member(s) can actually do this task?

- Do you have a checklist or chart to show your family member(s) how you want this task completed?

- Is everything clearly labeled?

DISORGANIZED FAMILY MEMBER(S)

To set up successful organizing habits in your house, you want to cater those habits to the most disorganized person in the house. From my experience, when someone in the home is "disorganized," most of the time it's that they have a different idea of what being organized means than you do.

If you have a disorganized person living in your home, you want to set up organizing systems that work for them. An organizing system is just a routine you set in place to give everything a designated spot or "home" within your home. It is basically an organizing habit that you put in place. Just like a habit you do for anything in your life, an organizing habit is a habit you do to keep yourself organized.

Let's review another example of an organizing habit you already do. You have a drawer for silverware, right? Well, every time you empty the dishwasher and put the forks, knives, and spoons away, you are following an organizing system you created. That system is the specific spot in your home you put your silverware.

You have many organizing habits already in place in your home. Where you put your towels is a habit. Where you store your bedding is a habit. Hanging clothes in a closet is a habit. The disorganized family member in your house also has organizing habits that probably aren't what you consider organized. I get that! But they do have a habit or habits, so you just have to find small ways to modify their habits to meet your organizing needs.

Pro tip

Be kind to yourself! Don't let someone else's definition of organization bring you down. We all have different systems that work for us.

I suggest starting with writing down what specific things the disorganized person is doing that bother or disrupt your organizing habits. Is it that they just throw their shoes near the door, making you trip over them when you come home? Do the items from their room creep into your hallway and down the stairs?

When you get specific about what isn't working, you can problem solve to create solutions to these organizational habits that aren't working. Some solutions may be easy while others may require some creativity. In later chapters, I cover in more detail some of my tried-and-true solutions to common organizing habits that I have encountered through my in-home organizing work. Here, I will give you an example for what to do with piles of paper on the counter, just so you have an idea of what I am talking about.

I had a client whose kids would always empty their backpacks and dump everything on their tiny kitchen island. The mom loved that they emptied things but got so overwhelmed with the piles that

she didn't know what to do. So, she had the kids stop emptying their backpacks in hopes that she would limit the piles of paper clutter. Well, after about two days she had to stop because she missed two permission slips and a class sign-up sheet. She went back to the drawing board to try and find another solution to this paper problem. She decided to purchase a rather expensive wall organizer to put the papers in. But guess what the kids did with their papers? They left them on the floor, which created an even bigger mess. This is when she called me and asked for my help.

After a rather quick consultation, I recommended trying a tray on the island where the kids could put their papers. It kept things tidy but also was something the kids could easily do and were used to doing. But by giving the papers a clearly defined space, the clutter reduced drastically because the papers had a designated spot or home. This solution meant looking at what the kids were already doing and simply tweaking what wasn't working. The papers being thrown on the counter with no designated space was the problem. Giving them a spot was the solution. At night or later in the afternoon, the mother would go through the papers in the tray so she wouldn't have any paper clutter, as that was her preference. And everyone won!

If you are the organized person, then you can adjust what you do while your disorganized family members will only have to tweak their actions. It is far easier for you to change your behavior than others who aren't interested in doing so!

Pro tip

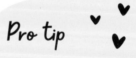

Another helpful way to modify a habit for a disorganized person is to watch what they are already doing and then create an organizational habit around their current behavior. This way you are making slight tweaks that are easy to follow.

I had a client whose husband would empty his pockets on their dresser in their bedroom. It bothered her so much because her jewelry would get lost in all the piles of coins, receipts, random paper clips, and his wallet. She wanted a solution. So, we looked at what he was already doing—emptying his pockets. But my client noted that his pants are hung in the closet. We placed a large bowl to collect all his pocket things in the closet on a shelf above where he hung his pants to see if it helped, and it worked! This wasn't a drastic change for him. This simple change for a "disorganized person" helped the family maintain order.

WAYS TO CHANGE ORGANIZING HABITS

I recommend not changing to all new habits at once because when you try to change everything, nothing ends up sticking. Make small changes to help you and your family find order. Find ways that help you stay organized and ways that you can teach your family how to be tidy.

Pro tip

Make small changes to your habits weekly or monthly.

By making small changes, you will keep those organizing habits going for much longer than if you changed everything at once. And if your family isn't totally on board with this plan? You start changing your habits first. Then you can slowly and gradually make changes for them. This way, you already have things in place for yourself and you won't get thrown off by the family not doing something. You set your habits first, so you are confident in them. Then you can simply modify what they need to do.

Also, write down your new habits. Write down all the steps you want to do to change those habits. Hang them up around your home so you can stay on track with the habits you want to create. I like to write down the habit or routine I want to follow. I write down each step in order. Then I make a few copies of that habit or routine and I hang it around the house in places I need to see it.

Let's say I am changing my organizing habit by cleaning up the kitchen at the end of the night. I would start my habit by checking to see whether the dishwasher was empty. Then I would write, *"1. Load the dishwasher. 2. Run the dishwasher. 3. Wipe off countertops. 4. Wipe off table. 5. Clean sink."* All those steps would be written down on one piece of paper that I would leave on our kitchen counter or dining room table. I would have that paper at eye level so I can see all the things in the order I want to do them. To make sure that I stick to the new routine, I would also place the new habit guide or checklist in all the areas that the checklist will tackle to ensure that I do all the steps. I would keep a sticky note on the dishwasher with two of the steps. I would keep another sticky note near the sink with another step. This helps eliminate all the overthinking that comes with changing new habits or routines.

So, get yourself ready with lists or checklists to help you when you change your habits. Then you can do the same for your family. This will ensure that they follow the flow you want them to complete and they can change their habits with visuals.

HOW TO STAY ORGANIZED WITH A FAMILY

We talked about setting expectations and organizing for the most disorganized family member. But there are some other strategies you can do to help build organizing habits for the entire family.

First, let go of the idea that organizing will look like it did pre-family. You know, back when it was just you, and you only had to worry about organizing your own things. You didn't have to worry about organizing anyone else. You could keep your closet hangers two fingers apart from each other and your shoes lined up nicely in your closet. But now, you have others inhabiting your space, so you have to make some adjustments in terms of order and tidiness.

Pro tip ◡

Schedule some time to "meet" with your family and talk about everyone's realistic expectations for their organizing habits. This will help you decide what will work for everyone.

Second, as I mentioned earlier, define what organizing means to you and what that means in your house. If you want that perfect Pinterest pantry, then you need to be okay with the fact that you may have to keep it organized yourself. If you want your child to have a tidy room, you need to explain that to your child. If you want everything to be put away after it is used, then that also needs to be defined. You need to get clear on what you actually want and need when it comes to organizing. And you have to set realistic expectations because sometimes you are going to have to tidy things up yourself.

Lastly, you need to look at how others in your family organize. You cannot criticize or judge them for their actions, just as they shouldn't criticize yours. You need to see what they are doing and find ways to get everyone organized.

How to organize a mudroom or drop zone is a problem that most families encounter. Someone in the family doesn't put their backpack and jacket back where they need to go so someone else trips over them every time they come in. Come up with a plan together by stating the problem: "I keep tripping on everything that is left by the door. What can we do so they don't end up there every day?"

List the ideas and find one that works best for everyone. One thing that has worked for countless clients is to ditch the cubbies and just stick with bins for everyone's stuff. Throw the backpack, shoes, jackets, hats, gloves, etc. into that bin. Yes, it may take longer in the morning to gather up everything, but the items are contained in one place. This is far more manageable than trying to create something that isn't necessary for what your family will actually do.

Let's take my husband as an example. He is not disorganized, but he does not have the need to put his clothes away after he wears them. This bothers me because I do not like piles of clothes on the floor. So, I simply put a laundry basket in the location where he would pile his clothes. Now, he has a place to put his clothes that "aren't clean" but "aren't dirty," which would typically be in a pile on the floor. Instead, they are kept in a hamper where only those types of clothing go. Just make sure that the plan is something you can stick with.

Not everyone's organizing habits are going to look organized to you. But if your child or partner is okay with it and it isn't getting in the way of your organizing habits, then I suggest letting it go.

Pro tip

Let the small stuff go. I know it is hard, but when it comes to organizing a family, sometimes the small things need to just be. Focus on the bigger picture, like community spaces that the entire family uses.

When you get really clear on what you want, your family will listen. Find a balance between what you envision as organized and what you can actually maintain with the family. They really are two different things, and it is okay to let some of the perfection go.

Organize Like a Pro

Now you are ready to create organizing habits for your whole family. Use this list to begin.

- Set your expectations in front of the entire family. They need to know what you want and why. If you feel better about things when the kitchen is cleaned up every night, then share that. Express your feelings to them so they know where you are coming from.

- Create habits that everyone can do. If you want a clean kitchen every night, set the expectation that everyone has to put their plate in the dishwasher or by the sink. These are things children at any age can do.

- Write down what you expect the family to do so they are clear on it. Yes, make rules if you have to. It will keep everyone on track, and you won't get upset!

- Make a checklist or a chart for the kids to do their habits consistently and make small habit tweaks as needed. Maybe they are responsible for putting away their laundry once a week and the rest of the time you can do it for them. Then you can build up to them doing it all the time.

CHAPTER 3

Age-Based Organizing

In this section, we are going to break down what tasks are realistic to expect from kids in different age groups. This information has been gathered through my own experiences, along with those of clients and research done through Montessori teachings.

I have been using different parts of Montessori teachings for years. You probably are too but don't even know it. Do you have your kids clean up their messes in the kitchen? Do you have child-size furniture? Do you keep books and artwork at kids' eye level? All of these are based in Montessori teachings. And the reason I love that is because it goes hand in hand with organizing, as everything has a specific place and children are taught that at a young age.

Montessori is a methodology of teaching that allows hands-on learning (letting kids do the work with lots of room for mistakes), self-directed learning (kids choosing how they are going to do things like organizing their bedrooms or play spaces), and working together (isn't that what being part of a family is about?).

Now there have been some ideas out there that this does not promote creativity because everything is so rigid. But I think it is the total opposite! When you have everything in its place, you are able to reduce the outside distractions and focus on innovation and creativity. You can easily grab art supplies to construct beautiful drawings as soon as you get inspired because there is no hunting and searching for supplies. They are where they belong, and you can find them in their place.

The reason Montessori and organization go so well together is because they both promote thoughtfully structured spaces that support order. And by giving your child expectations for how you want things to be set up, you are giving them the hands-on opportunity to try. When you let them create organizing habits for themselves, you allow them to take control over their environment and figure out what works best for them. And by working together, the entire family benefits!

BABIES AND TODDLERS

Babies and toddlers can definitely benefit from order. When they are able to easily find the toys they want to play with, and when you can easily pull things out for them, the day runs more smoothly.

To create order for young children, start with less stuff. Yes! You don't need all the things for babies and toddlers that advertisers might have you believe. Spend more money on quality toys rather than a lot of toys that are of cheap quality.

When you have less stuff, there are fewer things to organize. Typically, a Montessori classroom has limited things out, few items hanging on the wall, and a presence of calm in the entire space. Instead of having bins full of items, thoughtfully placed items are set on shelves for the children to explore. This promotes thoughtful play. It may be helpful to rotate toys more frequently when practicing the Montessori method.

To do this, I suggest storing items in bins in a storage area. Then you can rotate toys weekly or monthly depending on how your children are playing with the toys. This allows the child to become an "expert" at playing with one type of toy before a new one is introduced. Then it can be brought back into the space the following week. This switching of toys also limits overwhelm when it comes to choices for toys to play with.

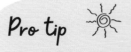

Pro tip

Don't solely rely on your kid's age. Children develop at different paces, so don't worry that much about age and think more about their ability level.

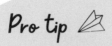

As the child develops more interests in exploring more things, try using real-life items instead of play items. Use wooden mixing spoons and metal mixing bowls rather than toy ones. That means less stuff you need to buy and less toys to pick up!

category. Maybe you have a child who loves dolls. You may have one basket for dolls. Or maybe you have one for the actual dolls with another for the doll clothing, and yet another for the doll furniture. Base the categories on the types of toys your child is interested in and wants to play with.

Watch your preschooler play with toys. See what types of things they are continuously playing with. Then look at what toys they never play with or are most often overlooked. Remove the overlooked and never played with toys. Keep the ones they always play with. Then group those toys into categories to help keep the toys tidy.

Now you can expect your toddler to put toys back on the shelves with minimal support. This means you can show them where items go, and they can maintain order with their toys. Since you don't have a lot of toys out, this process is perfect for teaching young children how to organize at an early age!

PRESCHOOLERS

As your child grows, continue to keep this system in place, but swap out toys with more time in between. Instead of every few days, try a week or longer. As the child grows, you can extend the amount of time an item stays on the shelf for up to a month before changing it out. But still keep the toys to a minimum! I know it is hard, and there may be other siblings who have their stuff as well. But when you have quality items instead of all the items, you are able to maintain order. I like to keep out a few categories of toys at a time. We can easily swap if we need to. But with a few categories, we are able to keep them tidy.

A toy category is a grouping of toys that go on a shelf or in a bin. Let's say your child loves cars. You can provide a basket with cars. That is one toy

Pro tip

Not sure whether your child still plays with a toy? Try this trick. Round up all the questionable toys. Place them in a bin in a storage area of your home or out of sight of the child. Set a reminder on your phone for one month from the date you removed the items from the play space. If the child requests that item, go grab it. After your one-month reminder, if the child doesn't request the item, you can confidently part with the toys in that bin.

For this age, I highly recommend picture labels for everything. Take real pictures of the toys and tape or Velcro them to the baskets or bins. When you swap out toys, add the label picture to the storage bin so you can just reuse it when you swap those toys into the play rotation again.

When we give our children the responsibility to do tasks that "grown-ups do" they continue to support the family with maintaining a tidy home. And you will see fewer tantrums because they feel like they are a "big kid" instead of a baby who needs everything done for them.

LOWER ELEMENTARY AGE

Lower elementary is roughly kindergarten to second grade. This group of kiddos can begin to have many more responsibilities in the organizing and tidying department. Let's start with toys. Children at this age can be 100 percent responsible for putting away their own toys on a daily basis. You may need a combination of pictures and text labels on bins. They should be responsible for putting things away because they are able to contribute more to the tidiness of your home.

To get the kids on board, create a checklist they should go through to be considered "done" with cleaning up. They may be working on an art project they couldn't finish or they started building with Lego bricks and they want to keep working on it the following day. On the checklist, include what to do with things they are still working on and how you want things placed in the bins or on shelves. This will support them in maintaining order with their toys and be able to pick up right where they left off.

They are also capable of sorting through their artwork to decide what to keep and what to recycle. I love doing this with families because when the parents see the kids sort through the papers on their own, I can visually see the burden of feeling overwhelmed by paper clutter being lifted from their shoulders. The biggest piece of advice when setting up organizing habits with paper is to give enough time from when the drawing/artwork was created to when you are sorting through the papers. This allows the child to determine whether what they have in front of them is their best work. Most of the time, the child will be able to identify their best work and the rest can go in the recycling. If they need support on this, you can help. Just remember that the less you do it for them, the more they will be able to do it on their own.

At this age, children should maintain a tidy bedroom. You will learn more about why organized bedrooms are game changers for decision making in the chapter on bedrooms, so it is really important that your child sleeps in an organized space.

Part of keeping a tidy room involves folding and putting away laundry. This can be done rather easily when all their clothes are stored together. Children in elementary school should be able to set up a dresser for their clothing as well, making putting away laundry an easy process.

I personally like the file-folding technique of folding clothes. This method is where you have the clothing standing up based on how you fold the clothes (the drawer looks like a filing cabinet, if you need that visual). The reason I like this method is because you can easily see each article of clothing. This helps kiddos pick out outfits without pulling all their clothes out of the drawer.

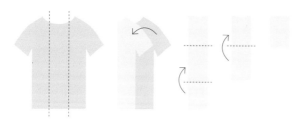

To file-fold, lay an item of clothing down flat. Let's say it is a T-shirt. Fold each side (about one-third of the shirt) into the middle. Then from the bottom, fold the T-shirt to the middle. Again, it is about one-third of the shirt. Then fold the bottom up again. Place the T-shirt in the drawer standing up. I like using drawer dividers or baskets because they help the clothing stand up.

At this age, children should help take out the garbage, clean up after meals, and help with outdoor chores around the house. It's best to teach children these skills when they are young, and then you can add more skills to their repertoire as they get older.

UPPER ELEMENTARY AGE

Upper elementary is about third grade to fifth grade. In addition to all the other organizing habits you are instilling in them, you can tweak some of the stuff they are already doing. And by tweak, I mean add or build on.

Let's say your kiddo is already putting away their own laundry. Maybe you can add on to that chore by having them get it out of the dryer and bring it to their room. Maybe you want help with dinner, so your child gets to do meal prep with you.

As the kids start to get older, the number of toys they are playing with starts to dwindle. This is a good time to reassess which toys they want to keep and which they can part with. This is where you need to let the child decide. Don't respond with "Are you sure?" or "Don't you want to keep this?" You are requiring them to do the work, so let them live with their decisions. If there is a sentimental item you want to keep, then take that item and say why you want to save it. Otherwise, let them have the final say. You will feel better once they start to take ownership of these things, so let them. As parents, it can be hard to let go, but we have to in order to truly let our kids learn.

Continue to build on the organizing habits you are instilling in the kids at this age. This will help them when they are grown up and living on their own because they will have these skills already instilled in them.

This is also the age that homework may start, so you will want to support them in creating an organized spot to work in your home. Have the children set up spaces where they can keep schoolwork or papers. Let them make the decision, but you can support them in creating their space.

The upper elementary age is a great time to start teaching time management skills. This includes planning for school projects and homework, being in charge of their own calendar of activities, and spending time with friends.

Pro tip

Be the example for your kids. If you want them to be better at time management, then show them how you do your planning. Maybe set up an afternoon where you can do it together. Walk them through your thought process so they can see it in action!

Sometimes natural consequences work best for children. Natural consequences are things that happen because you did or didn't do something. Let's say your child didn't plan enough time to get a homework assignment completed. The natural consequence would be a poor grade on that assignment. It can be hard to do, but it is something that will help your kids in the long run. So, you may need to take a step back and let them take charge of organizing their time.

MIDDLE SCHOOLERS

Middle school is a fun age when you can expect a lot more from your child. They can be responsible for cooking a family dinner, cleaning up the kitchen, and, most importantly, keeping their room clean.

Most middle schoolers I have encountered do not like cleaning their rooms—often because they never had to. So, I am giving you some tough love here. If you don't see the point in teaching your kids organizing habits at a young age, you are going to get middle schoolers who won't know or want to learn how to keep things tidy. That is why I am so big on starting early. Teach them while they are young. You can expect some mess because of the age, but you know that they have the skills needed to be organized.

If you are starting now, you are not too late. Anyone can learn how to organize. It just may take more time. Start by teaching your child how to fold clothes and create a system to store their clothing in drawers or in the closet. Don't fight them on

how they want to store their clothing. If they hate folding clothing, then hang them! Give them options, but don't try to make them do what you do. Let them decide.

Pro tip ✦ ◇

Ask your middle schooler what their idea of organized is. They know what they want. So let them share and know that you may need to manage your expectations about what organizing means in their room.

Once the clothing situation is figured out, then you can focus on other chores you are going to require of your child. Start small and build up. It doesn't help to "shock their systems" by doing too much at once. That is when they may rebel.

I have asked middle school clients what they want to be responsible for and they listed out things they wanted to do for themselves. When they say those things, let them! Give them 100 percent ownership of the tasks they selected.

I had a client whose child said she wanted to be responsible for all her clothes, including laundry, along with all her own meals for breakfast and lunch. Her parents agreed to step back and let her do those things on her own. After a week, the daughter didn't do laundry and didn't have an outfit for a school event. The parents didn't jump in. They just let her problem solve because she said she was responsible for those things in their house. After that incident, the parents told me that she started to do her laundry on Friday after school, before going out with her friends, and she has never not had an outfit for a school event again.

Natural consequences work, so let them happen. The world is not going to end, even though they may feel like it will. The lesson is far more valuable than a few days of preteen angst.

HIGH SCHOOLERS

I highly suggest treating your high schoolers like grown adults. They will be off on their own soon, so they need to start learning how to do things for themselves. If you haven't already gotten your high school child to participate in planning and cooking a meal for the family, then teach them these skills. They should be responsible for doing their own laundry, changing bed sheets and bedding, and cleaning up after themselves.

These years are going to be crucial for setting organizing habits they can carry with them if they go to college or live on their own. You want them to be successful humans, and to do that they need to know basic things like how to keep things tidy, do their laundry, cook, and clean.

Ask them to get involved in other household tasks. They can be responsible for grocery shopping if they aren't able to cook dinner. They can schedule their own doctors' appointments as they know their schedule best.

Pro tip ♡

Create a family schedule where you rotate household chores every day. You can make it fun and incorporate a chore wheel— whatever the spin lands on, that's their chore for the day.

You do not want to be the parent who makes "cheat sheet" cards for your child when they head off to college because they don't know how to do laundry, or fold their own clothes, or keep their desk organized. By teaching them organizing habits at a young age, your child won't be in shock when they have to live on their own.

Let me tell you an embarrassing story about myself. I never had to do my own laundry. My mom always did it for me. I would have to fold it and put it away, but I never had to put it in the washing machine or dryer. I knew where it was in our house, but I never pressed a button on either machine. So, when I went to college I waited to do laundry until I truly had no clothes left. I went into the laundry room of my dorm and looked at the machine. Then I ran out crying because I had no idea what to do. I called my mom and she had to walk me through how to wash clothes—every single step. I was eighteen years old. Do not let this happen to your children. Teach them how to do their own laundry when they are young so they will not be crying in a laundry room in a dorm basement like I did.

Organize Like a Pro

Use this list to help you and your child(ren) keep their spaces organized.

- Create a plan for what organizing looks like to you and your child.
- Ask your child what they feel being organized means to them.
- Get clear on your expectations and what they can actually do.
- Make a giant checklist for you and your kids to follow with a few tasks a week.
- Give them one or two tasks at once.
- Once they master their one or two tasks, add one more.
- Let them take charge of their calendar and their own tasks once they are ready.

CHAPTER 4

Overcoming Perfectionism

I've always been organized for as long as I can remember. I never had to do any "chores" because I would keep my room clean, my dolls nicely lined up, my desk tidy (with books stacked largest to smallest), and my clothes neatly put away. But with all this organizing came crippling perfectionism and the need to always have to keep everything tidy.

My need for perfection really kicked in as I got older and experienced some traumatic life events that were completely out of my control. I felt that I could no longer control the world around me, so I decided that I could control my bedroom and my stuff. Organizing became a way for me to maintain order in my life.

When I moved in with my husband, I learned to adjust my organizing habits to keep order in our home. Then our family grew, and I had to organize for an entire family of four plus a dog. And there I was, adjusting my organizing habits again.

As a mom, organizing is my way of saving my sanity in this world of motherhood. It is what I am good at. It is what I can do easily, with little to no effort. It is something that I can teach others. But with that is my underlying need to control and organize all things. If that sounds like you, you may be dealing with perfectionism.

You do things until they are perfect, even if that means sacrificing time with friends, family, or sleep. You are overly critical of yourself or your work. You are able to find the flaws in anything about yourself. Sound familiar? These are the obvious perfectionist tendencies. But there are also characteristics of perfectionism that aren't as obvious—those weird "quirks" you have that you can never pinpoint but hold you back from completing tasks or being happy with that you have accomplished.

× THE NOT-SO-OBVIOUS CHARACTERISTICS OF A PERFECTIONIST

Did you know that crippling procrastination can be a characteristic of perfectionism? Now, I know what you might be thinking: "Everyone procrastinates." And yes, everyone does, but the reasoning behind the procrastination is what distinguishes this as a characteristic of perfectionism.

Perfectionists get crippled with fear of completing a task if they don't think they can do it perfectly. So, they put off completing the task for as long as they can. This can lead to projects not getting completed, goals not being met, and dreams not being executed because they keep pushing off starting, or stopping at a specific step because it isn't perfect.

Another not-so-obvious characteristic is having an all-or-nothing mind-set. This fits nicely with procrastinating because a lot of the time, perfectionists believe that they either have to do all of the projects, tasks, and so on, or they will complete nothing. They believe that if it cannot be done perfectly, then they won't do it at all.

Perfectionists have a hard time looking at the growth they have made in reaching a goal. Again, this goes along with the all-or-nothing mind-set. Our focus is solely on the goal, not the process. By taking that personally, perfectionists can be more prone to depression and anxiety. This can be super tough because we can feel unsuccessful for not meeting said goal. But we need to flip that and focus on the growth.

Now this was 100 percent me back in the day. I would get so discouraged when I didn't meet a goal, say, for when I was teaching. My principal would set these benchmarks and we would be "graded" on them. If I had a student who struggled or needed extra support, I would work so hard to provide that. But if the test scores didn't reflect that, I got a lower "grade" on my benchmark. This led me to get frustrated and resentful at work. Instead of focusing on all that I had accomplished for all the other benchmarks, I would fixate on this one that I basically had little control over. I started having very high anxiety around testing and curriculum planning that I burnt myself out of teaching altogether.

Another not-so-obvious characteristic of perfectionists is being highly defensive of our work and personal traits. This can lead to low self-esteem since we, perfectionists, tie our worth to achieving our goals and providing work that is of high standards.

Going along with my story above, after years of these poor benchmark "grades," I started getting defensive of the work I was doing. I would question everyone else and their teaching methods. It led me down a path that I really didn't need to go. This is why I want to share how you can power through perfectionism. You can learn to get through some of these characteristics to be the best *you* can be!

Now what does this have to do with organizing? I know you have been asking yourself that. Well, if you are a perfectionist, creating order in your house can be challenging. You may want to make everything perfect all the time and you may take it personally when someone puts an item in the wrong space. Or you get resentful of others in your household for not taking care of things like you want them to. To help you with some perfection tendencies, I have some helpful tips.

HOW TO OVERCOME PERFECTIONIST TENDENCIES WHEN ORGANIZING

Start by looking at the differences between what is your standard and what is your reality. They are two totally different worlds. It takes a lot of time to get there, but it is possible. As I've mentioned, it is really important to get clear on what organized looks like in your home.

To see the difference between these two, start with what you want. Like what you really, really want (you should be singing Spice Girls right now). Ask yourself the questions on page 141 to get clearer on what you want your home to feel and look like. Then read through them as you look around your home. You will start to notice that what you wish for and what is reality are two totally different things. And that is okay! You can want things tidy and "perfect" but still functional for everyone living in your home.

Nothing is perfect and no one expects you to be. Organizing is not perfect; it's what's functional for you and your family. If there's something you want to change, go for it, but if not, know that it is okay. This is where managing your expectations comes into play. Know what is real versus what you wish for.

So, the first tip is to let go of one thing that isn't "perfect" when it comes to organizing. Let's say you don't have all matching hangers in your closet and it bothers you so much because the closet isn't "perfect." I want you to sit with the mismatched hangers for a day or two and try not to go buy new hangers. Let the space just be; those hangers don't matter. Your closet is still organized.

Pro tip

Try letting go of small things.

Another tip is to give someone else a job and let them do it all the way without you jumping in. This could be letting someone else load the dishwasher or fold the laundry. Let them do the entire job by themselves and don't interject or help.

Sit with that for a little bit, as it will help you let go of some of your perfectionist ideas so that you can actually take some things off of your plate. That is the goal with these tips—to allow others to help in the organizing of your home. It shouldn't all fall on you. And while you may enjoy doing some of these things, it is okay to let others do them too. When you let others help, like your children, you are actually teaching them skills that they need to know. You don't want them going off to college or out into the real world without some basic life skills.

Pro tip

Hide or remove yourself so you aren't hovering over your family member. Try not to go looking for what they did wrong. Just let them do the task at hand.

I have been told that over time my perfectionist tendencies will not be as strong, but I have yet to see that happen. However, what I have learned is that I can live with things out of place for one night. I can live with things that are not tidy for short periods of time, which is a huge improvement from when I was living on my own.

I've had to change my ways so that I could live with my family. Otherwise, I would have run away a long time ago because not all of my family members have the same definition of organizing as I do. Learn to let some small things go and you will start to notice some of that perfectionist pressure lifting from your shoulders.

SMALL THINGS TO LET GO OF NOW

- Hangers that don't all match
- Pantry baskets that are not all the same color
- Toy baskets that may be put back in the wrong place on the shelf
- Tasks that other members are in charge of doing (if they completed the task, try not to spend time trying to "fix" it to your liking)

✦ THE UN-PERFECTIONIST

Now let's say you are the opposite of a perfectionist. You are an un-perfectionist. You are disorganized and you want to get organized. What do you do then?

We will get really philosophical for a minute because I want you to understand that organizing just means to "arrange things in a systematic way" according to the dictionary. So, to be organized, you just have to arrange things in a way that makes sense. That could mean that you may already have things in a way that makes sense to you, but not to anyone else in your home. So, you feel like you are disorganized. Or maybe you have been told all your life that you are disorganized but when you actually look at it you have a creative mind, so your systematic way looks different than it does for others.

THE UN-PERFECTIONIST CHECKLIST

If you do one of these things, chances are, you are organized.

- ◯ Put away items in the same place.
- ◯ Order your items in a way that you understand.
- ◯ Have a system that helps you find your items easily.

We need to stop saying we are disorganized and lean into the fact that we have our own organizing habits that help us in our own way. I joke with my husband that he is disorganized. But in reality, his organizational systems are different than mine. Neither is right or wrong. Since he is a more go-with-the-flow type, I can put my organizing systems in place because they keep me calm. He is okay with that as long as he can keep doing some of his organizing habits, such as using a laundry basket for his clothes that are not clean and not dirty.

Just know that you are most likely already organized in your own way. And that is great! Keep in mind those pictures you see online are not going to be your endgame because you have your own system.

WHERE TO START WITH ORGANIZING ✄ HABITS

The first thing you should do is look at the habits you have now. What is bothering you or your partner or children? Is there something you can tweak to help everyone stay organized? If there's a habit that isn't working for everyone, then try to think of different ways to implement a change to those current habits.

One of my clients had adult ADHD and was constantly being told she was disorganized. Her purse was never where she thought it would be and she always lost her keys. After looking at her organizing habits, it was easy to see that she organized by doing what others told her worked for them, not what was already working for her.

She could never find her purse because she sometimes placed it on the kitchen island, while other times it ended up on the dining room table.

Instead of doing that, we found a basket near the garage door for her to put her purse and keys. It went right on top of the washing machine so nothing else would get piled on top. And it worked because she wanted her family to stop putting their things on top of the washing machine. So, by her keeping her purse there in a basket labeled "purse and keys," no one put anything in the basket because they knew it didn't belong. Her husband liked the idea, so he ended up putting his wallet and car keys in that basket too. They told me they have yet to lose the keys to either car because of that one little organizing habit.

It wasn't a perfect solution, but it was what that family needed. So, stop trying to make your home organized according to someone else's ideas and do what works best for you and your family.

Organize Like a Pro

Use this list to organize without perfectionism getting in the way.

- Look at what your and your family's current habits are.
- Ask yourself and your family members what you want to change.
- Figure out how you can make small tweaks to current habits.
- Create a master calendar or checklist for your family to follow.
- Delegate tasks with realistic expectations.
- Let go of the small stuff and focus on the overall goal.

CHAPTER 5

Letting Go of Overwhelm

Most of the time when I get a call from a client, it is because they have reached a point of overwhelm where they just don't know what to do or where to start. They have lost control of the situation and are now struggling with how to proceed.

It is totally normal to feel overwhelmed. Everyone does—even professional organizers. Do you feel that you are immobilized by overwhelm? Do you feel you simply cannot complete a task and cannot see the steps you need to accomplish said task? Do you think it may be your perfectionism taking over? This happens to me a lot. I get really overwhelmed and I cannot figure out where to start or what is a priority. In my mind, it seems like everything is a priority and everything has to be completed first thing, at high urgency!

When you feel too overwhelmed, you just have to start! Start by putting those scissors away. Just the scissors. Now you got your body moving and did something that was so easy. Start small. Start easy.

That paper pile on your counter is making you feel overwhelmed. So, start small. Recycle all the junk mail. You can easily see what junk mail is without even opening anything. So, start there. Once the junk is removed, start opening mail that could be junk, because those are easy to spot too. You know, the pieces of mail that say things like "open now for a great deal" or "inside you will find 10 percent off." Make a decision immediately: keep or recycle. If you do not need that thing right this instant, then recycle it. Sometimes just getting rid of it will motivate you to do more to keep things tidy.

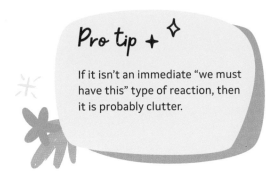

Pro tip

If it isn't an immediate "we must have this" type of reaction, then it is probably clutter.

Do something that you can do daily. If you see something that sticks out and gives you a bad reaction as you're looking for something to wear and scanning your closets or drawers, throw it in a bag that you can store in your closet. That bag is for things that you don't really enjoy, wear, or even like. By having a bag in your closet, you can easily find a place to toss clothing you no longer wear. If you do this daily, you won't have to do a giant overhaul of your stuff. You can simply declutter as you decide what to wear. By making small changes in your decluttering process, you will find that you're not as overwhelmed with doing a big declutter.

Breaking every step into small tasks can help you plan for completing smaller things instead of completing one big thing. It makes the tasks feel more doable, makes you feel like you completed something, and helps reduce feeling anxious or overwhelmed thinking about that big thing you didn't or couldn't finish.

NO PLAN, ALL OVERWHELM

What if you get overwhelmed and cannot even break down tasks? You get that crippling feeling where you just have no idea where to start. You are struggling to find anything around you that feels right. Or you see the piles of things and you just cannot deal with all the clutter. You may have started to clear things but have no idea how to proceed.

This is a common thing I have seen and experienced as well. I have learned that you have to just keep going. I know that isn't earth-shattering advice. Pick up an item. Throw something in the trash. Take a short break by setting a timer.

It really does help to set a timer when you get overwhelmed because you can do anything for fifteen minutes. Set a timer and tell yourself you have fifteen minutes to declutter that giant pile. You don't have to do it all. Just for fifteen minutes. Then you can take a break. Again, set a timer for your break and then come back to the task. Keep doing this until you have cleared your clutter or completed your task.

Setting time helps limit the overwhelm. So does taking a new perspective. When I get overwhelmed and stuck, I get up and walk around with a specific purpose to find something to focus on. When I find a new perspective for a space I want to organize, I ask myself to find something to:

- Throw away
- Sort with other items I have already found
- Donate

By looking at the items with a specific purpose, you feel like you are making a change with what you are doing. It stops some of the overwhelm because you are working on a new area with a new perspective.

Sometimes you just need to ask for help. That could be from family members, friends, or a professional organizer. There is no shame in investing in a professional to come and help walk you through steps to stop the overwhelm.

Explain as best as you can about how you are feeling, what is getting you stuck, and what is causing you to feel overwhelmed. The more detail you can share with a professional, the more they can help you.

A big habit I want you to get used to is to stop thinking of feeling overwhelmed as a bad thing when it comes to organizing. Accept the overwhelm because it is not going to stop you from moving forward. You are going to take action to declutter your stuff. You will find a way to get through the overwhelm and use that strategy on other organizing projects you complete. This will help you focus on your actual organizing instead of on the overwhelm!

Pro tip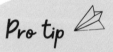

A quick online search can help you find a professional organizer in your area. If you can't find someone local, search for someone online that feels like they will "get you" and see if they can meet virtually.

Pro tip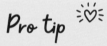

When you start feeling overwhelmed with clutter, take a quick five-minute break from organizing, then come back and pick one item to donate/sell/trash.

If you choose to hire an organizer and the organizer comes into your home, I highly encourage you to keep everything "as is." Do not "tidy up" before they come. And here's why. When you clean up for the organizer, they are not able to see how you use the space. Your stuff says a lot about how you use your space, so when the organizer can view how you use it, they can come up with ideas that will best serve your needs.

✦ ✦ ⧼ HOW TO ⧽ ✦ ✦
MOTIVATE YOURSELF

Figuring out the best way to motivate yourself isn't always what people want to hear. But it is what I have said earlier in this chapter—you just have to start! Start small and clean as you go. This method is probably one of the oldest methods for keeping things tidy. When you get up to move, like go to the bathroom or get a snack in the kitchen, bring one thing with you to put away in its spot before you do the thing you were planning on doing. The reason this works is because you are doing small tasks in correlation with a task you need to do. (See, small tasks for the win!)

Let's say you are working at your desk. You have to use the bathroom. So, you take your coffee cup to the dishwasher on the way to the bathroom. You just did a tidying task!

Maybe you are watching television. You want a snack. On your way to the kitchen, you have to walk through the dining room. In the dining room, you have some piles of paper that need to be recycled. Maybe it is some kids' artwork or notes that you are done with. So, grab those papers and recycle them before you get a snack.

By doing these small tasks you are keeping things tidy and aren't letting them build up to be giant piles of messes later in the day!

You can also use your decluttering time to multitask on something you enjoy. Let's say you love listening to music or an audiobook. Use that as motivation as you declutter something. When you multitask with a reward in mind, you are able to enjoy the process. Think about it. When you work out at the gym, do you watch TV while running on the treadmill? You are using something you want to do and enjoy doing with a task you may not be fond of. Maybe you enjoy baking. While your bread is baking, use that time to

declutter a kitchen drawer. You are able to multitask through an activity you love.

Another way to motivate yourself is to set a goal with a deadline. When I set a deadline, I force myself to meet that deadline because I hate not completing things. It is just who I am. So, if you are like that too, then set a goal with a deadline to have the kitchen decluttered or to organize your closet. Then set small tasks for how you are going to reach your big goal.

For example, say you set a goal to declutter your bookcase by the end of the month. So, you set a small task to go through one shelf a week. Then spend your week decluttering that one shelf—and only that one shelf—before you start to get overwhelmed by the entire task. That one shelf is your task. By the end of the month, you will have decluttered and organized your entire bookshelf!

When you set a goal and stick to it, you reduce the scary feeling of how big a project is and only focus on that one small task.

Organize Like a Pro

Use this list to organize without all the overwhelm.

- Write down everything you feel you want to organize.
- Do small tasks to get motivated.
- Clean as you go.
- Set a timer.
- Give yourself a deadline to finish a task.
- Move around to get a new perspective.
- If you are indecisive about an item, let it go.
- Multitask while decluttering. Add your favorite thing while decluttering (music, audiobook, podcast).
- Call a professional organizer for help.

CHAPTER 6

Mental Clutter

When most of us think about clutter, we probably think about external clutter, but clutter can refer to more than piles of laundry on the floor and dirty dishes in the sink. Clutter can also include mental and emotional clutter. Mental clutter is the clutter that is sitting in your brain. This overstimulation can feel as if you have a lot of different tabs open in your brain without one straight thought.

What does mental clutter have to do with organizing? Well, when you have a cluttered brain, it's hard to get things done and live in an efficient manner, leading to stress, low energy, or both. Mental clutter can lead to you feeling overwhelmed with easy tasks like emptying the dishwasher. Let's say you have lots of thoughts running through your head while you are emptying the dishwasher. You then struggle with where to put a kitchen utensil because your brain is being taken over by other thoughts. So, emptying the dishwasher takes longer than you expect it to, which can cause you to feel anxious or stressed.

On the other hand, if there's external clutter in your home, that can lead to mental clutter as well. It is like a never-ending cycle with clutter! Taking the time to find your keys every day or find your favorite shirt or a pair of shoes can take up a lot of time that could be better spent doing important tasks or having "me" time. Also, when you think of home, you want it to be your safe space. You want your home to be a place where you can unwind, but when you have lots of clutter, it can feel like the opposite.

So how can we clear the mental clutter? I have a few tips!

♥ WRITE IT DOWN ✏️

One way to clear mental clutter is to write down everything you are thinking. The reason why brain dumps work so well is that once you write it out, you are able to process the information and let it go from taking up space in your brain. A research study shared in the *Journal of Educational Psychology* found that when you handwrite notes you are able to process and synthesize key points more effectively than typing. And if we are looking to rid ourselves of the mental clutter, doesn't that make more sense for our brains?

Set a timer for ten minutes. Write down everything you are thinking onto a piece of paper. When the timer goes off, you can see all that was cluttering up your mind.

SCHEDULE TIME

Schedule time to sit with your thoughts. This will help you process your emotions and ideas in a more structured space. Start by setting a timer for five minutes whenever you don't have any distractions around you. Sit with either your eyes closed or open, your call.

Ask yourself how you are feeling. Really get into the feeling. Are you anxious about something? Walk yourself through why you are feeling that way. Are you overwhelmed with a task? Walk yourself through how you can break that task into smaller tasks, so you aren't overwhelmed. Then create a game plan for yourself. When you schedule time to really dig deep and get into how you are feeling, creating a plan on paper can help you remove that clutter.

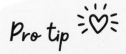

Pro tip

Add this mental clutter–clearing exercise to your morning routine! You can set your timer for five minutes before you start your day to give yourself a clear mind to focus!

🌙 GET MORE SLEEP ✦

When you sleep, your brain clears out things that it does not find to be useful, which means some of that mental clutter can disappear after a good night's rest. When you sleep better, you feel better. It is recommended that you get at least seven hours of sleep per night but shoot for nine hours to ensure you actually get a peaceful rest.

🔖 LIVE IN THE PRESENT →

Another way to reduce mental clutter is to live in the present moment. Stop focusing on things that happened in the past and stop worrying about things that could possibly happen in the future. By staying in the present moment, you are able to only

LESS SCREEN TIME

Another way to limit mental clutter is to spend less time on your screen. I know it is hard in a digital world, but studies show that reduced screen time has many health benefits. Avoiding screens before bedtime can help you get a good night's sleep too!

A study posted by Harvard shared that screens, especially social media and games, spark the reward system in our brain, making us addicted to our devices. Because of this we are not spending as much time processing our emotions and dealing with the mental clutter in our brains. So, reducing your screen time is crucial to clearing clutter.

focus on the things that actually make a difference and reduce feelings of stress. Living in the now helps you stay grounded and combat anxiety.

There is no need to worry about things that happened in the past because they have already occurred. You can learn from those events and change your behavior, so they don't happen again. But fixating on those events will not help you move forward. Don't spend time worrying about what the future will bring; it hasn't happened yet, so there's no need to stress about the unknown. Staying in the present helps you reduce emotional clutter.

MENTAL CLUTTER = PHYSICAL CLUTTER

Have you noticed that when your brain is overwhelmed your physical space is as well? There is a huge correlation between the two. When your physical space is not clear, your brain has a hard time processing things. And when your brain has a hard time processing things, your mind gets cluttered with too many things to process. It is like a roundabout with your car. If you stay in the inner lane, you just keep going in circles and cannot get out of the roundabout. This is like keeping your house filled with clutter. Your brain is going in circles and cannot get off to exit!

And as mentioned earlier, physical clutter also leads to mental clutter. When you have too much

Pro tip

Not sure how to live in the present? Look at your children. They do it all the time! They only focus on what they are doing at that exact moment. They aren't worried about what they are going to do in a few hours. They simply exist in the moment they are in. Try it! It's fun!

stuff in a room, notice how your body gets tense and you just want to close the door? That is your brain saying, "Nope. Not interested."

You want your space to be a place where you can relax, so by clearing out clutter you are creating a safe space for yourself to just be. When you get rid of physical clutter, you are less likely to have mental clutter clouding your brain.

I am not a morning person, but I found that when I am up early in the morning, even for thirty minutes before the family, I am more confident in what we are doing for the day. Whatever it is that you can do to clear some mental clutter, do it!

By taking time to deal with your mental clutter, you are going to feel so much lighter. You will be able to think more clearly and you will be more productive. You don't have all the clutter weighing you down when you are making decisions, thinking about tasks, or doing jobs around the house.

Pro tip ✦ ◇

If your physical clutter is taking over, start in places where you need the most "brain power," such as your office. Start there to keep your desktop tidy. Then some of that mental clutter won't be as overwhelming.

Organize Like a Pro

Use this list to keep all the mental clutter away.

- Grab a piece of paper and a pen and do a brain dump.

- Set a timer for five minutes and sit with your emotions. Ask yourself how you are feeling and why you feel that way.

- Get more sleep—at least seven hours' worth, but more can be helpful.

- Live in the moment and enjoy the present.

- Take a break from your digital devices. Try to avoid them an hour before bed.

- Reduce physical clutter. Try keeping spaces clear where you have to make a lot of mental decisions.

- Change up your morning routine. Allow time to get yourself mentally prepared for the day.

☀ CHANGE YOUR ❁ * MORNING ROUTINE ✦

One thing I found to help with mental clutter is changing my morning routine. Now why would a morning routine help with mental clutter? Let me explain. When I wake up before the kids—and yes, it is hard to do—I can focus on my to-do list for the day. And I can do a brain dump before they even wake up.

Changing what you do in the mornings might mean you need to wake up a little earlier to schedule your day. It might also mean that you start going to bed earlier to ensure you're getting more sleep.

CHAPTER 7

To Bin or Not to Bin

One topic that gets brought up a lot in the world of organizing is storage bins. Storage bins are used to contain items. The bins can be clear, wire, woven, or plastic. There are so many different bins out there, so this entire chapter is just about the idea of bins being a way to organize your things.

Some organizing experts suggest you get all matching bins to limit visual clutter. Other professional organizers say wait until you have decluttered, then buy bins. Yet other organizers say you may not even need bins to keep things organized at all.

If organizing experts cannot come to an agreement on bins, how are you supposed to?

In this chapter, I will break down how you can determine whether binning your items will help or harm you in changing your organizing habits. There are three bin approaches I will cover here: bins first, bins second, and no bins.

 BINS FIRST

The idea of getting uniform bins first, then organizing into said bins is based on the idea of "visual clutter." Visual clutter is when a space is overwhelming to look at. Your brain doesn't know what it should focus on, so you are spinning. This is typically seen in primary classrooms with bright colors and lots of "stuff" on the walls.

By reducing the visual clutter, you create a calming visual aesthetic for a space. Once you place the bins in their designated spots on shelves or in drawers, you fill them with the items.

Adding labels that look aesthetically pleasing is also encouraged with this method. All the labels are unified so that you are not looking at too many different things at once. Your brain is able to process what things are and focus on the words rather than trying to figure out what you're looking at.

The downside to this approach is that you have to find all matching bins first. That means that your stuff may not all fit into a bin in order to follow this approach, which could lead to things going in different bins or having to create an overflow area for extra stuff that doesn't fit. You also may find that you are simply containing your clutter: you are just throwing all of your stuff into matching bins with labels and calling it organized.

I have seen this all too often with clients. They end up getting matching bins that they find on sale. Then they line them up in their pantry or storage closet. Then items are simply thrown into the matching bins. When we spend time going through the bins, the clients quickly see that about 50 percent of the items inside the bins are not necessary for them to keep, such as old documents or extra batteries that the client was unsure were new or old. (After checking, they were all old.) Or garbage—wrappers from kids' fruit snacks that the kiddos stuck in the bin. Or Halloween candy that was supposed to be hidden but was forgotten about.

If you are the type of person who gets overwhelmed by too much visual input, are easily distracted by things and forget what you were looking for, or needs super simple systems, then the bin first approach may be for you. But if you do bins first, then you have to spend more time decluttering your items, so you only keep exactly what you need, instead of throwing things into the bins and calling it done.

When you spend time decluttering the items, then you can be sure that you are keeping only things that need to be saved because those items are things you need and use—not because you have room in a bin.

Pro tip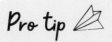

Keeping your clutter contained may be your definition of organized, so if this works for you, then that's great! But create a plan so that you avoid things being thrown in the wrong bins and just becoming clutter. Avoid those piles of unnecessary stuff and try to go through your bins once a month or so and remove unnecessary items.

✿ BINS SECOND ≋

The method to bin second requires that you first see what you have, then find bins to meet your needs. This involves a lot of decluttering and grouping before you even attempt to find containment for your items. This is the approach that I like to take with my clients because it makes them aware of what they have before we even approach bins.

In this approach, you start by completely decluttering your stuff. That means you go through every single item you have in a space. Let's say you are going to work on your pantry. You want to make it more functional for the kids to get their own snacks. So, you remove everything and sort through all the items you have in the pantry. You check expiration dates. You take inventory of what

items your family no longer eats, because we all know that kids can like something one minute and hate it the next. Then, you group all the items based on categories or on how you use them. For example, you can put all the rice together. Pasta and sauces can be stored together. Snack foods can be grouped together. You can sort all these items on your countertops to see what you have and how you want them stored in your pantry.

Then you go and find containment that works with the items you want to group together. These could be pasta containers with airtight lids, smaller bins to hold meal prep items, or shelf risers to store canned goods. Because you are not buying all the same bins, you are able to find organizing items that meet your needs in any given space. You have the flexibility to find storage items that work with your space and the things you want to store. The focus is on your stuff, not the bins you are using.

The bin second approach can create visual clutter, though. That means that you could have a bunch of different bins and containers that may not all look cohesive. As a result, you may find yourself being pulled into looking at something because it sticks out in the space you just organized.

I was helping a client in her beautiful pantry. She had all sorts of glass containers and bins that she was using to store baking items. I was just helping her organize the drawer spaces she had. But one thing I noticed was that my eye always went to this one corner where she had a tan bin instead of a white or clear bin. That tan bin just stood out from the other items in the pantry. So, we simply found a white bin to hold the items and swapped that white bin for a tan bin to store paper plates. And that one tweak totally changed where your eye went in her pantry.

If you use this approach, you can find things that make the space more cohesive by sticking with one color of bin. You just have to be mindful about the visual clutter if that is something that bothers you.

For me personally, I have found that this approach works best because I end up saving more time and money when I focus on decluttering first instead of finding bins first. I have found that when clients try to purchase uniform storage items, they spend so much time and energy on selecting matching bins rather than the work of actually decluttering and organizing. Thus, when it comes time to declutter, they are left with little to no steam. They end up only half-focusing on decluttering because they have no more energy left and are ready to be finished with the project.

Pro tip ✦ ✧

If you want all matching bins, you can still get that aesthetic with this approach. You just are able to get a clear idea of how many bins you need first.

NO BINS

The third approach to binning is to not use them at all. This idea is from the minimalist community. Minimalism is an idea that you only need a few things in your home. There is a wide range of minimalism definitions, as some minimalists say that living in a tiny house is the only way to be a minimalist. Others say that just owning fewer things is being a minimalist. Basically, you are living with only the items you need, and nothing more.

This way of living is not for everyone, but their approach is no bins. They are not things you need and since you are living with less, bins must go. What I have learned about not binning things is that since you only have a small amount of stuff, you don't need the containment.

If you are living like a minimalist, the items in your kitchen may include a limited number of kitchen knives and gadgets. This means that drawers and cabinets are not cluttered with stuff, so you do not need to contain them. The drawer itself is the container.

QUICK DECLUTTER CHECKLIST

Use this list to figure out what to get rid of.

- ○ Take inventory of everything you have.
- ○ Check to see if you have multiples of the same items.
- ○ Do you use the item?
- ○ How long has it been since you've used the item? If you don't use it, then it is probably an unnecessary item that you don't need.
- ○ Donate, sell, or throw away the item.

One family I was working with wanted to live a minimalist life. So, they basically had me help them downsize their entire kitchen. We got rid of about 60 percent of their kitchen items, including a vegetable peeler (that is one thing I couldn't give up!). Because they got rid of most of their kitchen items, we didn't need drawer organizers or bins because each drawer held only a few things. Each cabinet only stored a few items. The pantry was easy because we lined everything up like you would find at a grocery store, which meant that nothing needed to be stored in a bin.

But let's say you don't want to contain items in your pantry. You can easily store them like you would find at a grocery store. If you don't want bins in your closet, then hang all your clothes. Store items like you would find at a clothing store.

The no bin approach can be done if you are looking to just stop yourself from collecting too many things. By not having the containers to store your items, you are less likely to stockpile things that don't need to be piled. You are keeping things to a minimum because of the space you are giving yourself.

Pro tip

If you're unsure what to get rid of, take note of all the items you use for a month. Any items left unused during that month are most likely things you can get rid of.

Everyone has items that are necessary to them. I am not the one to tell you what you need and don't need. Only you can do that. You may not need gadgets in the kitchen when you have a knife. You may not require as many shoes because your clothing options are reduced. See how everything comes down to defining what organizing means to you? This is why it is so important!

⊞ HOW TO START →

In order to change a habit, you have to get clear on what you actually want to change. When it comes to bins and storage, I suggest looking at what is working in your current space, then creating more habits around what already works for you.

If you find yourself with too many places to "hide" things inside of bins, you may want to find an approach that uses fewer bins. You may find that lining up items like in a grocery store is easier than dumping all the boxes into canisters every time you go shopping. Thus, it's best to see how you can best organize and maintain your stuff before you buy bins.

Maybe you want to completely overhaul how you store things because it is too visually distracting for you. You struggle with finding clothing to wear because your eyes always go to the hangers of your clothing instead of the clothing itself. So, determine what is working for you, then set up more habits similar to the ones that are working.

Remember that there is no right or wrong way to use bins to store your items. You simply have to look at your needs first and figure out which option is right for you and your family.

Organize Like a Pro

Keep yourself organized and figure out whether or not you need bins.

- What does organization look like to you in this space?
- What do you envision an organized space looking like right now?
- Do you need bins to make this space organized?
- How will you use the bins?
- What are the categories you will create to keep your items contained?
- Can you keep up with this organizing habit you want to create?
- When you walk into this space, how do you want to feel?
- Do you get overwhelmed when you see many colors in one space?
- Does visual clutter bother you?
- Do you need all your bins to match?

CHAPTER 8

Labels

I am an over-labeler. The reason I am a huge believer in labeling is that it really helps keep the entire family organized. Because everything has a specific label, there is no second-guessing where something goes. When you spend all this time decluttering and organizing, why would you just leave the maintenance up to chance? With labels you are not! However, labeling can also be visual clutter to some individuals. While I love labels, it may not be the right thing for you. And that is okay! Find a way to make it work for you when it comes to labeling things.

If you have other people come into your home to help you with anything, they will know where things go if it is labeled. If you have family who want to help you after you hosted a gathering, they will know where things go. If you have family members with a different idea of what being organized means than you do, they can easily put things away because they don't have to think, just read. They can follow the organizing systems you have put in place.

Labeling is probably the easiest way to *keep* things organized. But what are some ways you can label? Now this may sound silly, but hear me out. There is a method to my labeling madness. There is a very specific way that I go about labeling all my things. The reason I have a specific way to label is because I want to make sure an organizing habit works first before I spend time labeling all the things.

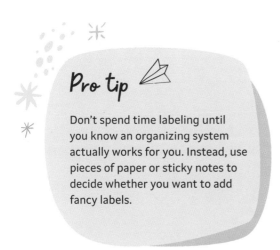

Pro tip

Don't spend time labeling until you know an organizing system actually works for you. Instead, use pieces of paper or sticky notes to decide whether you want to add fancy labels.

So, I start by organizing everything based on how I envision it in my home. I set up new organizing habits for my family. Then I use sticky notes to label everything. And I label more than just the regular stuff with sticky notes—I also include how to use a specific item with the sticky note. For example, if we changed where dirty laundry is to be stored, I would write on a sticky note "dirty clothes." Then I would write on another sticky note on a dresser drawer "put dirty clothes in basket labeled dirty clothes." I do this because we are changing a habit, so I want to make sure that all the steps are included for changing that particular habit. That is why I love sticky notes. They are the perfect way to change habits, because you can leave a path of notes for yourself to stop doing something and replace it with something else.

Once I have determined that the organizing habit is working, then I think about labeling that space in a way that is more permanent. There are so many options for labeling that it can be overwhelming in itself. I am breaking down which types of labels I enjoy using for specific areas of the home. You can use my suggestions as a guide to start.

LABEL MAKERS

I love using label makers for labeling drawers. Since the label comes out so small, you can add it to any drawer or drawer divider. This helps keep each section of the drawer organized. Some label makers even have arrows you can use to point to which section you are labeling. Here is how I use my label makers for each specific space.

Kitchen

I use the label maker to label the kitchen drawers, including the drawer dividers inside the drawers. This is mostly for the kitchen utensils drawer and the silverware drawer. I also use label maker labels for cabinet shelves and pantry shelves. You can use them inside the buffet on the shelves as well.

Bedrooms

I use the label maker to label every single drawer and shelf and area of the closet where things should go. For one client, I labeled the color of clothing that was to go in each specific section of her closet. This helped when she was putting clothes away. We added a label to the top shelf above where the hanging rod is located to label each section. I would also recommend labeling the shelves for shoes.

Toys

Sometimes a label maker is perfect for labeling toys if a child can read it. I typically recommend picture labels for toys because they are easy to understand, regardless of reading ability or language level. But I have used label makers to label toy bins. If you create an art cart, you can add labels to the cart as well.

Bathroom

Label makers are perfect for bathroom drawers and shelves. I think it really helps keep them organized. You can also use a label maker to label the inside of the drawer organizers. This helps items get back in the right place.

Office

I love using my label maker to label the drawers in my office desk and to add to any files that I may need to make. I have used my label maker to label clients' desk organizers that sit on their desk as well. This helps everyone keep the papers and office supplies tidy.

Mudroom

I call the area where shoes, jackets, and backpacks are stored near the "exit" door of your house a mudroom. It can also be called a drop zone. You may think you need a giant room with cubbies for it to be called a mudroom, but I don't believe that. You can add labels to each spot for shoes, backpacks, jackets, sunscreen . . . you name it! You can add labels to the shoe organizers so everyone in the family knows what goes where.

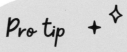

Pro tip

You do not need an expensive label maker to start making labels. Since there are so many options for label makers, find one that does what you need it to do.

♥ ♥ VINYL LABELS

Vinyl labels are labels that are cut using a type of craft cutting machine. I love using these labels for things that are more permanent. The vinyl labels can be expensive if you are buying them from someone or from a store. I have my own cutting machine, so I cut these for myself frequently. I just prefer the look, but you do not need vinyl labels to get things organized. However, since the labels can be tricky to remove, I suggest only labeling when you know the placement is final.

Kitchen

I use vinyl labels on the lids of my baking canisters. Since I have to store my baking items in a drawer, I need something on the lids that won't get messed up by the kids. The vinyl labels are the best for those items. But if you switch out baking items in your canisters, you may want to use things like a label maker or wine pens, which I talk about later in this chapter.

I also use vinyl labels on our fridge and freezer. I have all the drawers and side compartments labeled so that when someone wants to put things away, they know where it should go. That way, we don't have to worry about things getting shoved to the back and being wasted. I hate wasting food.

Bedrooms

I use vinyl labels to label the kids' drawers and bookshelves. Since I was not changing where those items go, I felt that vinyl labels were a pretty touch to those spaces.

Toys

I am a fan of vinyl labels for labeling toys for older kids. My kids wanted all their Lego bricks organized by color. So, we labeled each bin with the specific color in a vinyl label. The kids love it, and I can keep the Lego bricks organized by storing them in the correct bin. I also use vinyl labels to label shelves on art carts.

Bathroom

The bathroom is a great place to add the more permanent vinyl labels. Since you may not be changing out your bins as frequently in the bathroom, adding vinyl labels will be the perfect option to keeping things organized while also looking pretty. I used vinyl labels for my makeup, hair products, and hair accessories drawers.

Laundry Room

I love glass jars with vinyl labels for storing items in my laundry room. Things like dryer sheets, dryer balls, Epsom salts, and cleaning products are all stored in jars and labeled so I know what goes where and can find things easily.

Garage

I have our entire garage organized with vinyl labels. I told you I was an over-labeler! So, the pegboard in our garage has labels for each item that is to be hung on each hook. I did this so that if something is missing, we will be able to identify the item. It also helps when we are working and need to find something quickly. Let's say my husband shouts that he needs the tree trimmer. While I may not know what exactly he is looking for, the label will tell me what it is so I can grab it.

Pro tip

You can remove vinyl labels by using your blow dryer. The heat from the blow dryer makes the vinyl less sticky, so it can peel off easier. Put the blow dryer on high heat, low power. Heat the label by swirling around the blow dryer. Typically, it takes thirty seconds for the glue of the vinyl to lose its adhesive power. Try peeling it off. It should remove easily. This also works for stickers on bins too!

PRINTABLE LABELS

Printable labels are another great option for adding labels to anything. When I first started organizing, I didn't have a fancy machine or a label maker. I just had that printable label paper I got from the paper supply store. I used those to label clients' drawers, and they worked great! They do take some trial and error to format and print, but they are an easy solution. I would label the exact same things using the printable labels as I would with the label maker.

Now there are also ways to create custom-looking labels using printable label paper. There are so many options out there and ways you can create them. You can do a quick online search for free printable labels as well. You can find pantry labels on my website (see page 160 for the link)!

PICTURE LABELS

BIN CLIPS

Picture labels are just labels that have pictures on them. I use these for playrooms mainly, but I have also used them in bedrooms and mudrooms. I prefer real pictures for picture labels because they are more concrete. This way, a child can identify exactly what's in the picture versus a cartoon picture where it may be unclear.

To get the best picture labels, follow these tips:

1. Take a few items out of the bin or place the item that is on the shelf on a piece of white tagboard or lightweight cardboard. You can find tagboard at your local craft store.
2. Place the tagboard and those few items near a window.
3. Clean off your phone camera.
4. Take pictures. You may need to crop the picture to make sure you get it in focus for when you print it out.
5. Save the picture to a folder on your phone called "picture labels."
6. Repeat until you have pictures for every bin and/or shelf.
7. Print out all the pictures from that folder on your phone.
8. Laminate the pictures using either a laminating machine or just laying clear packing tape over the picture to protect it.
9. Punch a single hole in the top of the picture, then add a ring clip to the picture and onto the bin. Or tape the picture to the shelf using packing tape or add Velcro to the back.

Bin clips are probably one of my favorite organizing items. They are just clips that go on bins to help keep them organized. These are great for when you can't see what is inside, like woven baskets or lined bins. The bin clips come in a variety of sizes as well. They are great to add a touch of beauty to a bin.

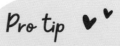

Pro tip

You can find bin clips almost anywhere! Do a quick search online and you can find a bunch of options. Just make sure you read the reviews to know the quality before you purchase. Not all bin clips work for the type of bin you may want to use it with.

Linen Closet

If you are not someone who likes to fold those dreaded fitted sheets, why not store your sheets in a bin instead? Add a bin clip to that bin and things are organized but you aren't spending time folding that sheet. Instead, you can just shove it into a bin and close the lid.

Mudroom

One of my clients wanted to have a basket for each of her children's shoes. We found sturdy baskets and added bin clips with each child's name. The bin clips were perfect because as the kids grew, she could just remove the clip from a smaller basket and add it to a larger basket when the time came. No need to relabel things.

Living Room/Family Room

I love decorating with baskets. So, in the living room or family room, adding baskets is a no-brainer for me. I add bin clips to the bins, so we know what is inside because I think it looks cleaner than just using a clear bin.

Pantry

I use bin clips in pantry areas as a way to help keep certain items together. I once had a client who wanted a bin for "meal prep" to keep her family's food supplies for the week. I found a bin, but she didn't like that it was clear. She wanted something more natural looking. So, we ended up finding a hyacinth basket and added a bin clip to keep "meal prep" items together.

Wine pens are my favorite thing to use when labeling those canisters or bins that are used often while also being changed frequently. These pens can write on containers and be scrubbed off without leaving a residue. Since they were designed to label wineglasses, they work best on glass and plastic.

Kitchen

I use wine pens to write on my glass Tupperware for leftovers. I write the date we put the leftovers in the Tupperware, so I know when it expires. I also use wine pens to write out what items are stored in our snack drawer. I keep some snacks on hand for the kids, but since it is a drawer, we need to see what is inside by writing on the top. This helps because we can swap out what is inside the container whenever a new snack comes in.

I also use wine pens to write recipes for things like oatmeal or pancakes on airtight jars. This way I can make sure the flours stay fresher in the airtight jar

and still have the recipe at hand. I use a wine pen to write down the measurements for flours as well. You can also cut out the recipe and tape it to the jar.

Bathroom

I use wine pens to label containers of things for the kids. For instance, if we travel, I use the refill travel containers and write down what is in each container. It washes off over time and with use, but it is easy to redo.

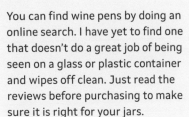

Pro tip

You can find wine pens by doing an online search. I have yet to find one that doesn't do a great job of being seen on a glass or plastic container and wipes off clean. Just read the reviews before purchasing to make sure it is right for your jars.

Organize Like a Pro

Labels make it easier to stay on top of things. Go through this list to keep things tidy using labels.

- Organize everything based on your vision.
- Set up organizing habits for you and your family to follow.
- Use sticky notes to label things.
- Once you are sure an organizing system is working well, then begin to use actual labels.
- Decide how you want to go about labeling items and space.
- Make sure labels are easy to understand and follow for family members.

CHAPTER 9

Bedrooms

Organizing your bedroom is the first thing I always recommend tackling before you do anything else. I am sure you are asking yourself, "Why in the world would I tidy my room before any other area in my house? No one sees my room, so why am I focusing on this one area first?" Well, sweet friend, there is a lot of research that shows when your bedroom is tidy, you get a better night's sleep. Your brain is able to go into REM sleep and sleep deeper. But what does that have to do with starting in your bedroom first?

Well, think about it like this. Let's say you start in the kitchen where everyone sees the stuff, but you aren't getting a good night's sleep. You start decluttering that space but are not 100 percent convinced that an item should stay or go because you are groggy and tired. Your brain isn't fully functioning because you didn't get all your REM cycles. You start getting rid of too many things that you later regret, so you stop with the whole declutter thing and your house turns into an episode of *Hoarders* because you can't figure out what to keep and what to part with.

Now, I totally did exaggerate the end, but you get the idea. If you aren't in the right brain space, meaning good sleep and rest, you aren't going to be as efficient with decluttering. So that is why we start in the bedroom first.

Pro tip

Try to get more than seven hours of sleep if you are planning on doing a giant declutter the next day! Your brain will thank you.

Do not worry about organizing the rest of the items that are leaving your room. We will cover that later on. Our focus right now, in this moment, is to clear off your counters and only keep things you use or cherish.

For me, our dresser has a vanity tray that was my grandmother's. On that tray we have perfumes along with a spot for my husband to drop his change and wallet. I also have my jewelry box. The rest of the dresser countertop is completely empty because I like it that way.

I keep the book I am reading along with hand lotion, a lamp, and an alarm clock on my nightstand. My husband has his alarm, lamp, and a diffuser we sometimes have on. But that is it. We don't keep a lot of extra stuff out because we really want our room to feel calm. By limiting what we bring into the bedroom, we are able to maintain that tranquility within the room.

TOPS OF THINGS

The very first, and often easiest place, to start decluttering in your bedroom is the tops of things like your nightstand, dressers, and any other area that may collect stuff.

Now, I don't believe that every counter should be empty. I just don't think that's realistic. So, I suggest figuring out which items need to stay on the countertops. Then make sure everything else goes to a different location within your home. The reason is that your bedroom should not be a dumping ground for things you don't know what to do with.

Your bedroom should be a retreat, a tranquil space where you can unwind. And you can create this tranquil space by taking control of the visual clutter that is on your dressers, nightstands, and any other top areas in your bedroom.

QUICK COUNTER DECLUTTER CHECKLIST

When looking around your room, ask yourself these questions to find that visual clutter on the tops of things:

- What sticks out when you do a scan of the room?
- Can you remove the items that stick out?
- Is your nightstand full of stuff? Does it need to be?
- Can you remove more things from the dresser/nightstand to clear more clutter?

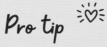

Pro tip

If you aren't using an item in your bedroom, but feel you have to keep it there for space reasons, find a way to make it not such an eyesore. Maybe try a storage bench for items that you use only occasionally.

FLOOR CLUTTER

Those piles of clothes on the floor or those books stacked in your corner of the bedroom? Yeah, they need to go!

Not only does the counter clutter affect your sleep, but so does the clutter that is piled up on your floor. So, it is time to come up with a plan to limit that floor clutter.

The first thing I recommend is to look at what is piled up on the floor. Do you have piles of work things you haven't had time to sort? Are there books you have been meaning to read? Piles of clothes? Workout equipment you never use? Once you figure out what the piles are, you can create a designated place for those items. Let me give you some examples.

The workout equipment that is hiding under your bed is either being used or it is not. If it is being used and is working in its spot in your bedroom, leave it. If it isn't visually pretty to you, maybe find

a basket or a bin it could go in. But you do not have to do that. If that pile serves a purpose for you, then let it be. But if it doesn't, that is where you need to declutter. If the workout equipment isn't working in your bedroom, think of another area in your home to try. Maybe the family room or basement? Test it out there to see whether that space increases your usage of the items.

The piles of work papers and/or books should have a better home than on the floor. Maybe you need to add a bookcase to your bedroom in the space where you have the books and papers piled up. Maybe you just need to pick up those piles and put them where they belong. Maybe you need to carve out a space in your home for an office or a library.

Clothes clutter on the floor can be tricky. Sometimes the clothes clutter can be from a lazy partner or child. Other times, the clothes may not be totally dirty, but you feel funny putting them back on the hanger. They are like those "in between" clothes that can hang out on a chair or floor because they aren't dirty but aren't clean.

Maybe that pile of clothes has to go to the dry cleaner. Or is it all dirty clothes? Or clean clothes? As you can see, there are so many possibilities as to why the clothes clutter is there. Which is why I said clothes on the floor can be tricky!

For the clothes piles, I suggest having two types of laundry baskets: one for dirty clothes only and one for clean clothes only. Here's the reason why. Let's say you are doing a load of laundry and have the laundry basket in the laundry room. You fill it with clean clothes. But a kid or your partner comes in with dirty clothes. They see your clean clothes in the hamper, so they throw their dirty clothes on the floor. The pile of clothes just gets bigger and bigger with dirty clothes. Then clean clothes start spilling over into the dirty clothes pile and then you don't know what is clean and what is dirty.

Now say you do a load of laundry and your partner comes in with dirty clothes. Guess where those clothes will go? In the dirty laundry basket, regardless of whether you have clean clothes in a basket or not. Now you won't stress about dirty clothes getting mixed up with clean clothes because you have two different laundry baskets. Problem solved!

But what do you do about the clothes that are neither clean nor dirty? They have just been worn and can be worn again, but someone in the family won't put them away. That is when you add a basket to hold those in-between clothes.

In-between clothes are usually the clothes you change into after work. They aren't dirty because you didn't wear them all day, but they aren't clean because you have worn them a few times already. Or it's the pair of jeans you just wore today but you don't want to put back because you are wearing them again tomorrow. By having a designated spot for those clothes to go, you are stopping that crazy pile of clothes on the floor!

Pro tip

Label the baskets so your family knows which basket is which or get two different color or size baskets to create a visual for what is cleaned and what is dirty.

QUICK FLOOR DECLUTTER CHECKLIST

Limit floor clutter by doing the following:

- Look at piles on the floor and find out where they belong that is not in your bedroom.
- If the pile has a purpose for you in your room, leave it. If it doesn't, remove it ASAP.
- If you have piles of books, try replacing with a bookshelf.
- If you have piles of work documents, try finding space in your office area or create an office space in your dining room.
- Create a plan for your "in-between" clothing.
- Make a laundry basket for clean clothes and one for dirty clothes.

✦ * CLOSETS AND
✱ DRESSERS

Another giant area of clutter can be your closets and dressers. Clothes can be incredibly hard to declutter, especially for women. Our bodies change so much from carrying children to aging to just style changing. So decluttering clothes can be rather sticky.

We feel guilty for parting ways with things we have loved in our "previous life." And by "previous life" I mean before kids/marriage/etc. We also feel guilty if we get a gift from a loved one, but the item of clothes may not be our style or taste. Parting ways with clothes that don't fit you or that you don't truly

love is going to be the only way to clear your closet of clutter. And it can be overwhelming if you haven't tackled it before.

Now I do want to note that if you are pregnant, do not do this next step. Just skip to the next section right now. If you just had a baby a few months ago, do not do what I am about to suggest. In fact, if you had a baby within the last year, do not start decluttering clothes until your child is walking. Just don't. You do not need to get upset about something as silly as clothes when your job is to care for yourself and your child. That is way more important. But the rest of you can totally do the next steps for decluttering clothes. And we need to be totally honest with ourselves as we do this. So, make sure you are ready; this won't be easy, but it will be so rewarding once you do it!

So many of us have some items that we hold on to, not because it looks good on us, but because of the memory behind it. This is where we have to separate the memory from the actual physical item. Sometimes it is as easy as trying on that particular item. You can see it isn't your style, doesn't fit, or isn't flattering. If that is the case, then it can be easier to part with it. Other times it can be more challenging. In order to declutter your clothes, you will probably have to try them on. This is a great visual for you to see whether something looks good on you or whether you are ready to part with it.

I had a client who had two full closets with tons of clothes. Her drawers were spilling over. She had nicely folded piles of T-shirts and workout clothes on the floor because she couldn't fit any more clothes in her drawers. Her stuff started to take over her husband's closet. And that is when they called me to help. This client wanted to organize her closet so she could fit all her things in her two walk-in closets. Her husband wanted his closet back. We started talking and it was revealed that she was having trouble finding things to wear. So, we started going through things that were hanging in her closet.

Most of the items hanging up were her pre-kids clothes. I asked why she was still holding on to these items and she told me that she felt she may one day wear them again. After some tough conversations about whether she was really going to wear a black strapless silk romper, she said no but it was just too hard to let go because she felt she was giving away a piece of herself. And this was the root of why she had so many clothes in her closet. She felt those clothes were her identity, her way to reconnect with memories of her past.

Only put back the clothes you know you wear. These clothes that are going back are a must keep. Make a pile of anything that is questionable. When you have gone through everything, then you go back through the questionable clothing.

Try on those questionable pieces of clothes. If they fit you but there's something off, try creating an outfit with those clothes. Add jewelry or a headband. Try to create an actual look with that piece of clothing in question. If you can't, then that is a good indication that you can part ways with that piece of clothing. If you do create an outfit, test it out. If you find out that you don't love it, then that is another good indication that you should part ways with it.

Start with a drawer or a section of your closet. Do a quick look through. Anything you know you can get rid of, do that. Then remove all remaining items. As you start to put things back, if anything looks questionable—anything that is a maybe or you are unsure about—keep it out. Only put the things back that you absolutely love and wear.

Continue this process of taking out a section at a time. The giant pile can be overwhelming and can stop you from truly doing the decluttering work you want to tackle. So do drawer by drawer and part of closet by part of closet. You can use the dividers in the closet to be the section you complete for each step.

I always suggest keeping a bag in your closet for things you don't want. It can be a donate and sell bag. Store it in your closet somewhere that is easy to drop something into. Any time you put on a top or pants that you just don't love, dump them into the bag. This gets them out of your closet quickly without you having to make a pile of clothes on the floor to move to another area of your home. When the bag is full, put it in the car to donate.

Pro tip ☼♡☼

Put back clothing you wear all the time first! Then, get rid of anything that doesn't fit or you don't like.

The reason I love doing the questionable clothing last is because you have seen everything in your closet. You know what you already put back. So, when you are trying on the questionable clothing, you are able to recall which items you could create an outfit with since you just put them away. And you are already tired from all the other work you just did. Making the decision to keep or get rid of something is much easier because your brain is ready to be done.

From my experience, the questionable clothing is usually not worth keeping. Every now and then you will have an item that you want to keep because it has meaning. I found that this is typically with baby clothes, but sometimes it is with your clothes as well. And if that is the case, I suggest creating a sentimental box to store those special items in (see page 124 on memory boxes). Each family member should have their own box. Store only the truly meaningful pieces. You can keep it in your closet or storage area. Just make sure you can access the bin when you need to put away a special item.

I have held on to the outfits my kids came home from the hospital in. I also have their baby blankets. My husband has a box with his letterman jacket and jerseys from his high school sports days. We only keep the items that are truly meaningful. Everything else we are comfortable donating or selling so someone else can enjoy them.

Now it is up to you to declutter your bedroom to get a good night's sleep. This will help you make better choices, be more decisive, and declutter more things, so you can create a calm and inviting bedroom for yourself!

Organize Like a Pro

Go through this list as you declutter your bedroom.

- Keep dressers, counters, and nightstands clear from unused items and clutter.

- Find a new space for items that do not belong in your bedroom.

- Have a laundry basket for dirty clothes and another one for clean clothes.

- Create a system for in-between clothes (and the floor doesn't count).

- Keep a bag in your closet for any clothing you no longer want to keep (declutter as you go).

- When decluttering your entire closet, do one section at a time.

- Only put back items you know you will wear.

- Keep questionable items out and decide on them after everything is put back.

- Make your bed.

CHAPTER 10

Kitchen

Another area of the home that can easily be overtaken with clutter is the kitchen. They say that the kitchen is the heart of the home, which is why most people see an increase of clutter piling up in the kitchen area. Since we spend so much time in the kitchen, whether it is eating, cooking, or doing homework, kitchens see a lot of traffic. This can cause the kitchen area to have a lot of other things pile up that are not "kitchen related."

One of my clients wanted a total transformation of her kitchen. She said she needed the space to act as a functioning kitchen and also serve as an office. I loved that she was realistic about all that went on in her kitchen. So we created different areas for all those different purposes within her kitchen.

Her kitchen was long and narrow, so we kept all the kitchen items near the sink and oven. The cabinets that weren't in the "cooking area" (near the sink or oven/stovetop) could act as an "office" space.

This is a great example of focusing on what your kitchen needs to do for you. But how can you actually go about decluttering the kitchen space, so you aren't collecting clutter and making the space take on too many "jobs"?

KEEP WHAT YOU NEED
⌒ x x x x ⌒

The very first thing you need to do when working in a kitchen is to only keep the stuff you actually need. I know it can be tricky, especially if you have a lot of space to store things. But clutter piling up on counters and in drawers is a real thing.

Let me tell you a story. I was helping a client unpack from a move. As we were unpacking, we quickly found out that she had four vegetable peelers. We found that out because we stuck all the vegetable peelers together. When I showed her the drawer with all the peelers, she said she had no idea she had so many. We found out that her old kitchen was not easy to keep tidy because it was long and narrow and had very few drawers. So, she would have trouble finding things. Or so she thought. As we unpacked more things, we found more duplicates or triplicates of things like apple slicers and bagel cutters. I suggested that she pare down what she has in her new kitchen to keep things organized. She kept two peelers, so her kids could help with food prep. We kept one bagel cutter and donated the apple slicers because she never used them.

After a massive declutter and full labeling of every single drawer, she was happy with the kitchen. A few months later, I checked back in to see how things were working. She told me that not only was her entire kitchen still organized like we set up, but that she hadn't had to buy any new kitchen gadgets because she could easily find the ones that she uses. She actually enjoys cooking now, which she said she used to dread in her old kitchen.

When things are organized, it makes life easier. When you can find everything easily, you are able to enjoy whatever task you have to do. I really don't like cooking. It is just not my thing. But when I have to cook dinner because I have kids that need to eat, the task is more tolerable because I can find everything I need inside my kitchen.

So where should you start with organizing your kitchen? I suggest making a giant pile of everything that is in your kitchen. Seriously, everything. Clear out every cabinet and drawer and spread your stuff out for you to see. Clean every single drawer and cabinet. When your drawers are all nice and clean, you are more likely to put back only the things you need rather than shoving everything in.

You have two options that are both effective. It is just a matter of which works best for you. The first option is to use sticky notes to label each drawer and cabinet with items that you want to go inside them. The second option is to go through all the items you have and pull out the ones you never use or can store in a different area of the house.

Pro tip ✦ ✧

If doing a giant kitchen declutter is overwhelming, start by decluttering one drawer. Take everything out of that one drawer and only put items back that you use. Make a list of what is in that drawer. Use that list as a reference to find duplicates of kitchen items as you declutter more drawers in the same manner.

Pro tip 🌿

If you find yourself with duplicates or triplicates of items, try labeling your kitchen drawers with what belongs in them.

OPTION 1: LABEL FIRST

To do this option, you are going to use sticky notes to label each drawer and cabinet with the items that you want to go inside that drawer or cabinet. Use the checklist on page 67 to go through each kitchen category to help you start labeling your kitchen items.

This option works best if the giant pile of stuff is overwhelming you or if you prefer to make a plan, then carry out that plan. This option is how I work with clients for moves. It helps give you a visual of the types of items you need. It also helps when it comes time to decide whether an item should stay or go. If you are writing down each type of category for kitchen items and you don't include one, that could be a sign that you don't use that type of item often, if ever, and that could be an easy signal that the item can go!

There are also some drawbacks to labeling first. For instance, if you forget a category—say, grilling supplies—and you need a large drawer because you grill a lot, but you've used the drawer for other items, you may have to redo everything to fit those items in a drawer or cabinet.

Once all the drawers and cabinets are labeled, you are going to start on one end of the kitchen and work your way to the other, putting things into the drawers and cabinets you assigned. As you are putting things away, start pulling out items you don't use or no longer want to store in the kitchen. Now you may be asking yourself, "What items wouldn't I be keeping in the kitchen?" Well, let's say you have gravy boats and turkey basters you use only during the holiday season. And you don't have a lot of cabinet space, so you might store those items in an airtight bin with your holiday stuff since they are only used once a year. This way, they aren't taking up space inside a drawer or cabinet in your kitchen, but you still have them in a place with items you use them with.

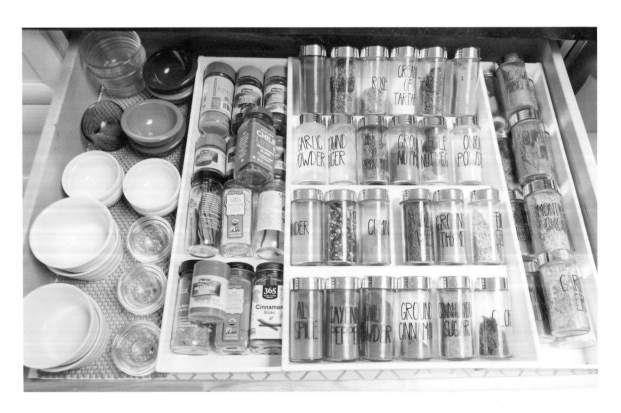

Pro tip

As with your closet, put back the items you use regularly first. For anything that is left over, decide whether you need to keep it in your kitchen or whether there is another place for it to be stored.

Once all the items are put away, you may find yourself with items that are left over. They are "homeless." If that is the case, you need to ask yourself whether those items are truly worth saving.

One client had all of her grandmother's china, including teacups, serving pieces, and platters. She also had her own china, including teacups, serving pieces, and platters. And she had her husband's grandmother's china, including teacups, serving pieces, and platters. Needless to say, they were set for a giant tea party even though no one in the house drank tea. These items were all in the "homeless" pile after we put away everything in her kitchen and pantry area.

When asked what she wanted to do with them, she struggled at first. She really felt that she needed to keep them, but we had no place for them to go. She said she never used them and wasn't interested in displaying them since she didn't like the pattern. So, we found an incredible organization that teaches etiquette lessons and donated all the teacups and serving platters. After donating these, we found room to store some of the platters that the client enjoyed. This is a rather extreme example, but there are ways to keep items that have meaning without feeling guilty because that is typically what happens to those leftover or "homeless" items.

Stop feeling guilty. You already spent the money on that item. You already appreciated the piece when it was given to you.

KITCHEN CATEGORIES

Almost every kitchen I have helped organize has these categories listed below. There are always other categories of items, but these are the ones I see frequently.

- Silverware
- Plates
- Bowls
- Platters
- Serving trays/fine china
- Serving utensils
- Cooking utensils
- Mixing bowls
- Baking items
- Pots and pans
- Cutting boards
- Baking trays/baking dishes
- Drinkware
- Tupperware
- Baggies/parchment paper/plastic wrap/tinfoil
- Cleaning supplies
- Towels
- Oven mitts/hot pads
- Spices
- Grilling supplies
- Small kitchen gadgets (hand mixer, immersion blender, garlic press, lemon juicer)
- Kitchen appliances (blender, slow cooker, air fryer)
- Food/snacks/meal prep items

DRAWER DECLUTTER CHECKLIST

When labeling all the drawers and cabinets first, follow these steps.

- ○ Grab sticky notes.
- ○ Write down each category of items you have.
- ○ Add those sticky notes to the appropriate drawer or cabinet.
- ○ Remove all your items into one giant pile.
- ○ Start putting items back into drawers or cabinets based on the sticky notes.
- ○ Donate/sell any items you no longer need or use.

Pro tip

Remember what organized means to you when organizing your kitchen. Use that as your guide for deciding how you want things to look and feel.

One client I had enjoyed baking and cooking and had all the gadgets. We started grouping items together based on what I thought was logical and how she would use the items. Well, I learned rather quickly that that was not how she used some of her items. She shared that she liked to keep all the things she uses for baking together, including the flours. Since this is how she used her items, that is how we stored them. There is no right or wrong way to store things. It just has to make sense to you.

Group your items by how you use them. Don't get fancy. Just keep it simple. This way, you can find everything you need when you need it and can easily put it back where it belongs. This will prevent you from buying unnecessary items because you can find what you need. Once the items are grouped together, use sticky notes to label the appropriate cabinets and drawers.

OPTION 2: PULL UNUSED ITEMS OUT FIRST

Another option for figuring out what you need is to look through your entire pile of kitchen stuff and pull out what you never use. This option is great if you don't know all the categories of kitchen stuff you have or if you are stuck on where to start. Since you are just going around and looking at your stuff, you can get an idea whether things are worth keeping.

After you remove items you don't use, group the items that you want to keep together. Since this is your kitchen, there is no right or wrong way to group things.

Pro tip

If it's easiest, group your common everyday products together. Do what makes sense to you and is realistic for your family.

One way to figure out how to group things together is to stand at the stove and pretend to be making a meal. Then ask yourself what items you need and where you would grab them from. For instance, if you need to grab a spoon to stir, where would you grab it from? Wherever you go is where you may want to store the spoons. Stand near the dishwasher and pretend to empty it. Where would the plates go? Cups and glasses? Water bottles?

When you visualize where things go in your kitchen, you have a better idea of where you should keep things. Sometimes it is easy to think that just because you have always done it one way it is the way your brain is trained to go. But you will be surprised when you reach for something that is in a different spot than you think.

Pro tip

You can use this visualization technique as your guide for where to store items in other rooms of your house as well! For instance, if you need help sorting items in your in-home office desk, imagine grabbing an item you need as you are working and then store your desk supplies based on how you visualize yourself using them.

When my husband and I redid our kitchen, I stood by the stovetop to think about where I wanted things to go. My husband is left-handed, and I am right-handed. Why does this matter? Well, if you think about how you would reach for things if you were left- or right-handed, it makes a difference. So, setting up the kitchen was a challenge because I do most of the cooking, but my husband enjoys it way more. We made some compromises. But we did this by each of us pretending to cook in the kitchen and visualizing where we would reach for things.

Take the sticky notes you created and place them in the spots you think you want those things to be stored. Then you can put the items away. But as you are putting things away, I want to ask you to not make a junk drawer. Whatever you do, do not create a junk drawer anywhere in your kitchen.

KITCHEN DECLUTTER CHECKLIST

When pulling out unused items first, follow these steps.

- Go through each drawer and cabinet to remove items you never use.
- As you are pulling items out, start writing categories onto sticky notes.
- Put sticky notes on cabinets and drawers by looking at where you reach for things as you pretend to cook.
- Make sure the remaining items are the category labeled on that sticky note.
- Tidy up the drawer.

NO JUNK DRAWERS

I have a major problem with junk drawers. I think they are totally unnecessary. They serve no purpose. And they take up a very useful drawer in your kitchen, so why are you wasting it on junk?

Okay, so my real problem with junk drawers is that it is simply a drop zone for your indecisions. That is what you are keeping in your junk drawer—things you are waiting to decide whether they are worth keeping or not.

Don't believe me? Let's go take a peek in your junk drawer. Now I am sure you have some useful things like pens and paper, right? Well, those aren't the things I am talking about. Because if you had an entire drawer for pens, paper, markers, and other office supplies, then that drawer is no longer a junk drawer but an office supply drawer or stationary drawer. Totally different purpose because everything in that drawer is being used, correct?

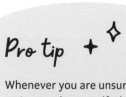

Pro tip

Whenever you are unsure about an item, ask yourself when was the last time you used it. If it's been a long time, then it's probably not a necessary item and it can go.

REMOVING YOUR JUNK DRAWER CHECKLIST

Want to get rid of the junk drawer for good? Follow this checklist.

- Remove everything from the junk drawer.

- Clean the drawer because my guess is it is super dirty.

- Give the drawer a specific purpose: office supply drawer, stationary drawer, tools drawer.

- Group items from the junk drawer together.

- Put back the items that need to go in the drawer based on its purpose.

- The items you don't know what to do with need your decision-making power:

  • Why are you holding on to this item?
  • What purpose does this item have?
  • If you throw this item away (or donate it), what will happen?

Typically, in a junk drawer, you keep old credit cards and long-forgotten keys. You keep chopsticks or sauces from takeout orders. You keep scrap pieces of paper with notes you don't remember. Gum and candies make their way into that drawer, sometimes leaving a sticky goo all over your stuff. These things are serving no purpose.

When you have a drawer that just collects things for you to figure out what to do with later, you are just postponing decision making. And that postponed decision making is costing you space in your kitchen and space in your head. The junk drawer is helping no one.

TOO OVERWHELMING?

The very best way to declutter and organize your kitchen is to dump everything out. If you can get yourself to a place where you can handle the overwhelming feeling, I promise it will be worth it!

But what if you just can't take everything out? What if you just freeze with the overwhelm and cannot do it? Or you start taking things out and feel a real panic attack about to take over. Or you don't have the time to take everything out because of babies or toddlers taking over your house. That is totally normal and happens to so many people. If that is you, I have a few ways you can still do the giant declutter without getting overwhelmed.

The first option is to do one drawer at a time, but you have to write down everything that is inside that drawer. I suggest numbering the drawers and recording what is inside that drawer so if you see something that you feel is a duplicate, you can reference your paper that has all the items listed.

Another way is to do only one category at a time. This could mean that all bakeware is sorted and then put away. By doing categories, you are still able to round up all the items that fit in that category and declutter what you don't need without emptying every single cabinet.

And the third way is to go through each drawer and cabinet and get rid of anything you don't use or have touched simply by looking inside the drawer or cabinet. This way of decluttering works best if you have all your drawers already grouped together by category. It really is a great way to declutter quickly once you have the foundation of order in your kitchen set up.

✧ PUTTING THINGS BACK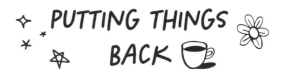

One thing I have observed with clients is how to put things away in an orderly manner. I have had clients buy expensive organizing bins and items only to find out that those items don't work in their drawers or cabinets. They did this because they thought that buying the items would be the solution they needed to keep themselves organized. And I have to say that the actual organizing items aren't going to be the answer to keeping you organized in your kitchen. The items may help you keep up with the organizational system you created, but they aren't going to be why you are organized.

Before you run out and buy all the organizing bins, let's take a step back and evaluate how to find ways to put things back where they belong in an orderly manner that everyone can follow. Once you've decluttered your kitchen and decided where things should go, then you can put things back.

Pro tip

Delegate tasks and have your family help you if it gets to be too much.

And when I say put things back, I mean follow the bins second approach discussed earlier (pages 46 to 47). Once everything is put away, you can assess what you need to keep the items organized. I found this method is best for kitchen drawers.

Let's look at your cooking utensils drawer. These are items like cooking spoons, spatulas, ladles, etc. You have all those items in a drawer without any bins or organizers. As you lay out the items inside the drawer, you see that it could use two drawer dividers. That is it. So, you measure, order, and boom!—your drawer is now organized. Don't buy bins until after you declutter and put away. It will save you time and money because you can find bins and dividers and organizers that work with your stuff rather than making your stuff fit into something it shouldn't. Maybe you find you are more of a minimalist than you thought, or you realize you don't love the location of the items. Getting products after you organize will help you analyze what you truly need.

PUTTING THINGS BACK CHECKLIST

Follow these steps to help you put things back easily.

- ○ Resist the urge to buy bins or drawer dividers.
- ○ Put items into the drawers or cabinets you decided based on the sticky notes.
- ○ Assess the items in the drawer or cabinet.
- ○ Decide whether you need a bin or drawer organizer.
- ○ Measure the drawer or cabinet.
- ○ Find organizing products that will work with your stuff in that drawer or cabinet.

SEASONAL KITCHEN ITEMS

There are some kitchen items that are totally seasonal, such as holiday cookware. If you have room in your kitchen, store holiday items in your kitchen. However, most people don't have the space to store these items in the kitchen or don't remember they are in the kitchen, so they end up buying new items, not using what they already have. My goal is to help you use what you have. Declutter the stuff that doesn't need to be in your home and only keep what you use.

Seasonal kitchen items can be stored where you keep your seasonal decor. I try to keep holiday platters and plates with some of my holiday decor. That way, when I get out the decor pieces, I am able to also take out the kitchen items I will need for that holiday. I do suggest keeping your seasonal items in airtight bins and using the dish storage bags to hold those items, so they don't break or get dusty. And you should always ask yourself whether those items are worth keeping. For items you only use once a year, I suggest creating a reminder for yourself. Maybe you add a piece of paper to the bin or bag as a reminder to see if you used an item this holiday season. As you are unpacking your decor and kitchen items, you can look at your note to see whether you do actually use that item.

Let's say you have a platter from years ago and you look at it this holiday season and realize that you haven't used it the past few holidays. Why are you keeping it? It is obviously not a serving piece you use because if it were, you would use it for the holiday. You use your favorite things during the holidays, and whatever you don't use isn't a favorite. Remember that.

It is okay to let go of things that once served you. You do not need to feel like you have to keep everything.

Sometimes you have to remember that a particular item served its purpose for you and now you can let it go.

Items that are no longer serving you are holding you down because they become clutter. That clutter is what is keeping you from having the house of your dreams—a space that is calm and inviting and full of your favorite things, not things you feel obligated to keep.

Pro tip

Do not feel obligated to hold on to holiday kitchen items if you never use them. Donate to a local organization that can give someone else the opportunity to enjoy that item for their holidays.

CHINA AND SERVING PIECES

People usually have a hard time letting go of china and serving pieces, mostly because these items are handed down like a trophy from generation to generation. You may get guilt-tripped into keeping your mother's china or a serving platter that came when your family immigrated to where you are living now. Whatever the reason, these items can easily take up a lot of space in your home. And that can mean two things: either they are useful and beautiful items you display, or they end up as clutter.

It can be difficult to let go of things you have an emotional connection to. Sometimes you may feel like you have to keep an item because of the sentimental value placed on it by a family member. No matter what the reasoning is, you need to look at the actual item and decide whether it is worth keeping. This is so hard. I am not trying to underplay how difficult it is to part with things that have sentimental value. Some things that I have found helpful when letting go of those sentimental items are listed on the next column and page.

Pro tip ☺♡

Sentimental kitchen items can be hard to part with. There is an emotional connection to pieces placed by either you or family members. Try removing the emotion regarding an item. Ask yourself, "If this were just a _____(ex. teacup), would I keep it?"

Only keep what you use. Only keeping what you use is helpful because you know that the items you are holding on to are actually functional. When you look at your china and serving pieces, pull out the items you use. Then the remaining items you can feel confident parting with. The reason being is that your house is not a storage unit. You want to keep the things you find useful stored in your home. Everything else can be stored elsewhere, not in your home. Maybe in someone else's home who will actually use it.

Ask the family. One thing that has helped me with clients is to have them ask their relatives whether they want a particular item from, say, Grandma's china collection. I have had countless clients say that someone in their family had a particularly fond memory of an item. By giving it to a family member, it doesn't feel like you are getting rid of it, and your family member can now enjoy something that you don't have to store in your home.

When asking family members to come and collect the items, set a pick-up date. This will create an urgency with that family member to collect the item so you aren't holding on to their sentimental item any longer.

Find ways to display your items. When you are able to display the things from your family, it makes them more meaningful. I had a fond memory of my grandmother's teacup collection, and when she passed, I took one teacup from each of my grandmother's sets. She had three or four sets. Then I got a teapot and coffee pot from my other grandmother. I have them on display in our kitchen. They make lovely decor pieces, and I am able to have that sentimental reminder of them without holding on to the entire collection of teacups.

Create a scrapbook. Another client created a scrapbook. She hired a professional to take pictures of the china. Then she found pictures of her family and extended family using those pieces at different holiday events. She turned the entire picture collage into a scrapbook that she gave to her family. It was a beautiful tribute to the memories those pieces of china meant. But she no longer had to hold on to every dish, platter, or bowl. You could even ask family members to write stories about specific pieces to add to the scrapbook as well.

Donate to a cause or find a local organization. Another option is to donate to a cause that is meaningful to you. There are also organizations (some of them probably local to your area) that host etiquette lessons to those looking to get into the workforce. There are also organizations that host tea parties for children with cancer or that are in hospitals.

Show gratitude but say no. It can be hard for us to say "no" when a family member offers to give us something sentimental. But just because something holds sentimental value to a family member doesn't necessarily mean it does for you as well. It is okay to say thank you but no thank you to an item your family feels is sentimental.

Back in the day, parents gave their expensive china to their kids because expensive china was a thing back then. Now, I can't name many people who register for china for their weddings. People may choose two types of plates, but rarely have I seen china on registries. And that is because we don't host fancy, sit-down, formal meals like they did back in the day. So, as our lives change, we can change what we keep as well.

Organize Like a Pro

When it comes to kitchen organizing, there are some new habits we may want to start.

- The first habit is to get everyone in the family to start putting things back where they belong after they have used that item.
- Label everything. The labeling will help everyone know where things go.
- Do a quick scan of items in your drawers or cabinets each time you open that drawer or cabinet.
- Look for items that are out of place and put them back where they belong.
- Look for items that you no longer use that are taking up space.
- Tweak the organizational systems you put in place so that you can easily access all of your things instead of just living with things the way they are.

CHAPTER 11

Shared Spaces

In this chapter, I am calling living rooms, family rooms, basements, sitting rooms, conservatories, and lounge rooms shared spaces. Every home has a different setup, so I am just lumping all those areas together into shared spaces because that is what they are—shared!

I love having an organized shared space because you can all be cozy together and not feel overwhelmed with clutter surrounding you. Whenever you have a movie night or are watching TV as a family, your mind won't wander to all the tasks you want to tackle in that room. Like the piles of paper on the counter. Or the books that are strewn about in the corner. Or that pile of boxes that are supposed to go to the basement but haven't made their way down yet.

The first rule to organizing shared spaces is to create organizing habits the entire family can keep up with. This means not creating anything that is super tricky, labor-intensive, or hyper-focused.

Super-tricky organizing habits are things that require you to be a more organized person than the average Joe. Let's say you want all your throw blankets rolled a rather specific way and stored in a particular manner. You prefer them rolled with the outside edges rolled in and you want them stored in a basket that is located on the other end of the room from where you typically walk to enter and exit the room. That is rather tricky, especially for younger kids.

Labor-intensive organizing habits are multiple steps to putting something away. Let's say you want all the remote controls to be stored in a box that is located near the television. So, you instruct your family to put the clickers in the box. But what you are not putting into consideration is all the steps they need to do to complete that one task. They need to get up and walk over to the television, then they have to take the lid off the box. The remote needs to be placed inside. Then the lid needs to be put back on. That is four steps to getting them to put away the remote. What is more likely going to happen is the remote will be placed on top of the box, hidden in a couch cushion, or just left where it was last used. Because there were too many steps, you made the organizing habit too difficult.

Hyper-focused organizing habits are where you need things done a very specific way. For example, if you expect your family members to karate-chop

the pillows after they sit on the couch, that probably won't happen. A karate-chop pillow is when each of the edges on the pillow looks like cat ears and it is "chopped" in the middle. I like my pillows like that, but don't expect anyone else to do it! Which brings me to how you can organize your shared spaces in a way that everyone can do.

HOW TO ORGANIZE SHARED SPACES

In order to organize a shared space, you have to think about how you want the space to be used. What often happens is we don't always give rooms a specific purpose. We just make assumptions as to what those rooms are supposed to be. But not every room needs to be used like it did when we were growing up.

Growing up, my family had a "formal living room" and a family room. The formal living room was never used. The television and comfy chairs were always in the family room. The living room had our piano that I stopped playing when I was in fifth grade. There was no place comfortable to sit. I always wondered why we had that room when no one ever went in there. Well, fast-forward to my husband and I house hunting and we came across a home with a formal living room and a family room. We were trying to envision what would go where. We ended up turning that formal living room into a playroom for the kids because we don't need a formal living room.

By rethinking what a room's actual purpose could be, you are then getting clear on what items should be stored in that particular room. Just because things used to be one way does not mean they have to stay that way. Start by giving your rooms a specific purpose.

Pro tip

Ask yourself, "What do I want to do in that room?" when deciding the room's purpose.

Some rooms are obvious, like a kitchen. But when you have multiple sitting rooms, you may want to be specific about each one. Is one room specifically for the kids? Is one room better for movies? Is one room a cozy gathering space?

For example, our front room was always called the living room because that was what was on the floor plans when we bought the house. But the room has always been the place we gather and watch television. So, we purchased furniture that would meet the need of gathering. We could have easily purchased formal furniture because that was what was on the floor plans, but instead we gave that room a purpose that met our family's needs. We also have bookshelves to store pictures and books that we enjoy reading, along with space to decorate for the holidays because we enjoy that as well.

DECLUTTER SHARED SPACES CHECKLIST

Stand in the room and look around. Use these questions to help guide you to decluttering and organizing your shared spaces.

- What do you want the purpose of the room to be?
- What is in the room that doesn't serve the purpose you want?
- What is in the room that serves the purpose you want?

After figuring out the room's purpose, you also have to be thoughtful about keeping that space organized so everyone can use it. Also be clear on what is expected from the family and what you are comfortable doing yourself to keep the room tidy.

GARAGE SPACES

Garage spaces are used for different purposes, but they are usually shared areas. I live in the Midwest, and we need to use our garage to park our cars during the winter months. But some families in other parts of the country use their garage spaces as living spaces. No matter how you use the space, there are some organizing steps you can follow to make sure it is a functional space for how you want to use it.

Select storage that helps you define the purpose of the space. Anything that doesn't fit into that purpose should not be stored in the garage. I suggest grouping items together by how and when you use them.

Pro tip

When organizing spaces for your pets, keep all their items together. Put food and medicines in one location. Toys can be stored together. This will keep things tidy for you and your pet!

One client had lots of tools to fix up an old car and had parts, tools, and other gadgets that needed to be put in order. We started by grouping all the things he needed for specific parts of the car. Then we grouped the tools he used. Once everything was grouped together based on how he needed to use them, we created storage for the items. We used heavy-duty garage shelving to add more space for tools that needed it. Other tools were sorted into a tool bench.

The family also had sporting equipment, so we put some of the equipment on the opposite wall from the tools and car parts. We created zones in the space so the family could use the garage for multiple purposes. Garages typically have three walls and the garage door, so you can zone off each wall to hold different things.

For example, maybe you want to use the garage for sporting equipment, storage, and yard items. Use one wall to hold all the yard items. Keep the lawn mower or snow blower on that same wall, just on the ground. Use the opposite wall to hold sporting equipment. Then you can add shelves to the ceiling to hold your storage items. Use airtight bins to make sure the items are protected when they aren't in use.

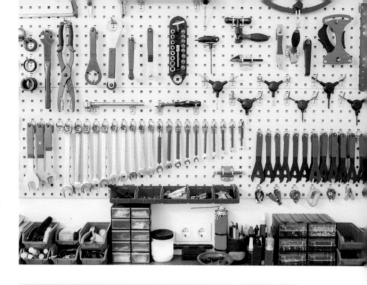

ORGANIZING YOUR GARAGE CHECKLIST

- Figure out its purpose.
- Remove items that don't go along with the garage's purpose.
- Create zones by grouping like items.
- Add shelving space, if possible.

Pro tip

Start with getting clear on what the garage space is going to be used for. Is it storage? Living space? Do you want to park car(s) in the garage?

YOU VS. THE FAMILY

Not all families have the same organizing habits, and that is okay. When you are setting up shared spaces, take into account what your family members will actually do to help keep the space organized. What are the things that you want and require of your family in that room?

For example, I do an end-of-night cleanup every night. I expect that the entire family will help out with this tidying session. I expect that the kids will pick up their toys and put them in the proper bins so they can find them in the morning. I expect all the cushions to be put back on the basement couch from the fort that they built that day. I also expect their jackets, shoes, and backpacks to be put away so they can get them in the morning and we don't have to search for things.

What I don't expect is my family to fold the throw blankets the way I like them. They try, and I leave them if they try, but I do not expect that to be done when I ask them to clean up our shared spaces. Instead, I fold the blankets, and I am comfortable with that. Find a balance between what you are comfortable doing on your own and what you expect other members of the family to do.

she was shocked by how much bigger the room felt. This chair was not that big, but because the chair's presence was a huge burden in the room, it felt like it took up more space than it actually did. We found a company that took damaged furniture and refurbished it to be used in a women's shelter. Her chair was going to a good cause, which helped her part with it. But she told me she didn't have any emotional attachment to that chair. She simply never thought to get it out of the room since the movers put it there when they moved in. This means that when you give your room a specific purpose, you may need to part with items that are no longer serving that room. That could mean donating, selling, or trashing items.

LETTING GO

Now comes the tough love portion of this chapter. A lot of times I have found that my organizing clients have items hidden in their living or family rooms that are not serving any purpose other than taking up space. They may not find something to be beautiful or useful or even functional!

One of my clients had a fancy chair that had a broken arm and it had been sitting in the corner of her living room for eight years. It just became a part of the room. So, when we removed that chair from the corner and moved around a few other items,

Pro tip

Try moving an item out of the room to see how the space feels. If something isn't useful to the room but has meaning to you, try it in a different room.

It is hard to part with items when you feel guilty about holding on to something that served its purpose years ago. This is where the tough love comes in. You need to stop holding on to things that aren't making you happy when you walk into a room.

Let's say whenever you walk into your living room there is a painting that was given to you by an in-law who is no longer an in-law of yours. You get angry seeing that painting because of the negative feelings you have from the crumbling of that relationship. You stop going into that room. But what if you just got rid of the painting? Or you painted over that painting with something new? Or you hired a local artist to transform that canvas because you like the size of the artwork? An easy fix can create an entirely new space simply by getting rid of or replacing an item.

WAYS TO GIVE ITEMS A NEW LIFE

- Paint the item.
- Reupholster the item.
- Move the item to a new room.
- Add decor pieces to make the item feel new.
- Use the item in an unexpected way.
- Repurpose the item into another useful piece.

There are a few ways to make simple changes to your space. You can throw away an item that doesn't fit in any room of your home. Putting it in the storage area for "one day" doesn't count unless you are waiting to purchase a home of your own and you have plans for it in the new space.

You can donate your item. A simple Internet search will help you find local organizations and a list of items they will accept. I suggest calling or emailing first just to make sure they take it. Write down the name of the person you talk to, because the pick-up people may have been told something different.

Repurposing or refurbishing an item is an easy way to change up your space to best meet your needs. One of my friends does this with pieces of furniture that she finds. She paints them or stains them or reworks them so they can fit into her home. She took a dresser and turned it into a console table by cutting out the bottom two drawers. She painted old furniture to give it a new look that she used in her daughter's bedroom. She also reupholstered furniture so the fabric matches her style.

If a painting or chair or book collection is not working for you or the family, you can move it, donate it, or trash it. It is your home, and you need to enjoy the spaces you inhabit.

Organize Like a Pro

Make shared spaces work for your family. Here's how to start.

- Get clear on what you want the room used for.
- Declutter the space and remove items that don't serve the room's purpose.
- Ask yourself what you want and require from your family to keep things tidy in that room.
- Figure out what you're comfortable doing in that room.
- Find balance between what you're comfortable doing and what's expected from your family.
- Don't hold on to items that don't make you happy when you walk into the shared space.
- Find local organizations to donate items you don't want.
- Repurpose items to best fit your needs.

CHAPTER 12

Office

Office organization is going to look a little different than organizing an area of your home, because not everything can be decluttered as easily. Some things may have to stay because they are work related. Some paperwork may not be easily turned into a digital document due to the sensitive nature of the document.

Maybe you work from home full time. Maybe you work from home a few days a week. Maybe you only work from home in the summers. Maybe your home office is your space to run and manage your household. The ideas I am sharing will work for you in any usage of your space. Just make sure to tweak some of the suggestions to fit the needs of your home office.

CREATING ZONES

We start organizing the office by looking at the physical space. Look around the room and figure out what the purpose of that space is. Most office spaces are for work, but is there another purpose for your office? I just want you to be realistic about what needs to happen in that space.

We are going to create zones. Zones are just areas of the room that are to be used for a specific purpose. These zones are going to help you keep your space organized. When you designate specific places for things to go based on how you use them, you are more likely to keep the areas tidy.

I am going to be more general here when I am talking about zones, but this is one area of your home that you need to get specific about its purpose. No office space I have ever helped organize has been the same.

I had a client who used her office as an art area for her kids as well. There were art supplies on her desk and on the table that was supposed to be used for artwork. Her filing cabinets were filled with art supplies. Her papers were stored on shelves near the art table. There were photographs, old artwork, recycling bins filled with empty bottles, and other items that did not belong in the office based on how the family used the space. Because nothing had a designated space, we had to create zones. Since the space was serving two purposes, we created zones to keep things separated.

We started by grouping all the art supplies and storing them on the shelves. Then we put all the papers in the filing cabinet. My client's desk was cleared so she had ample space to work. The kids had their art supplies stored somewhere that was easily accessible and near their art table. The items that didn't belong in either zone went to other areas that would serve them better.

Pro tip

If your office space is being used for multiple purposes, create zones for each purpose and section off the space to keep only those items in that zone.

There is no wrong way to create zones in an office space. You just need to figure out what you need for your space. When thinking about creating zones, make a list of all the things you have to keep in your office space. Then draw a room layout on a piece of paper as best you can. Break out the room into different zones and square them off on the paper, labeling the areas within each zone. After doing this, look at the furniture to see if you need to rearrange things to maximize your space. You can also see where you can utilize or add some shelving and storage space.

When you draw out the space, you are able to see how you can arrange the room to best create zones and use the space. This also makes it easier to figure out what needs to stay and what can go.

ONLY KEEP WHAT YOU NEED

Now that you have a specific purpose for your office and have created zones for the space, you can start removing items that don't meet the purposes of that room. For instance, if you are using your office only for work, then you want to store all work-related items and documents in this space. Work documents can look like household items, receipts, medical bills, and other papers you may need to file or store. Anything else that is not work related should be stored in another room. When you remove things that don't need to be in that space, you can make room for the things that need to be there so you can work.

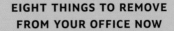

EIGHT THINGS TO REMOVE FROM YOUR OFFICE NOW

1. Junk mail
2. Broken items
3. Documents that you can easily access digitally
4. Miscellaneous cords or cables that you don't use
5. Old calendars and planners or notebooks
6. Excessive keepsakes, photos, or supplies
7. Old magazines, newspapers, or books
8. Anything that doesn't make you feel inspired

Pro tip

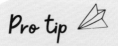

If you're having a hard time figuring out if you should get rid of an item, set it aside. If you haven't used it or needed it for a week or two, then it might be time to get rid of the item or remove it from your office area.

When I am organizing an office with clients, I have found that it is easier to remove everything from the space and then bring back items by placing them in their zones within the home office. Every item that is left out can either be thrown away or placed in a different location of your home because it doesn't belong in your home office.

FINDING A PLACE FOR THINGS →

Now all the items that need to be put back are in the office. But how do you find adequate places for all the things you need in your office?

Start with one zone at a time. I have found that the desk area is the easiest place to start because you know what you need to get to every time you are working. Set up the desk space so that the things you use daily are in desk drawers or on your desktop. Papers have a specific place to go in a file cabinet, filing box, tray, or magazine holder. Anything that doesn't need to be accessed daily should be stored in a different zone or drawer in your desk. Make sure you aren't just keeping items to keep them. Be intentional about what you are storing in your desk zone. These should be things you use daily or weekly.

Refill items can be stored in a different area or in a desk drawer that isn't at the top of your desk.

Once you have finished the desk area, start out with a different zone. Figure out how you want to store the next zone items. Maybe you need to move furniture. Maybe you need to invest in new furniture.

Whenever I am thinking about this, I like to pretend that I am doing the things I would do in that zone. Let's say you need to create a "shipping center" or a space that you can use to prep and store items for shipping or mailing in your office. Do the things you would do when you are packing up an item you are going to ship out. Where would be a good place to store the shipping tape? Scissors? Packaging?

Wrapping? All these items should be easy to get to and put away; otherwise, you won't keep up with it. Once you figure out where you would like things to go, find a storage unit or wall system that can work for what you need.

Since you acted it out, you already know what will and won't work for you. Don't get something just to get something. Find something that will work for exactly what you need it to do. Continue this process until all the zones have order.

OTHER THINGS TO CONSIDER

I do want to note that if you are only working in an office a few days a week, then it is helpful to set up your home office in a similar way to how you have your office desk set up. When your items are placed in similar locations, like all your pens are placed in a cup in both office spaces, you'll be able to concentrate more on your tasks and less on where things are located.

If you have to bring items back and forth from your home office to your work office, take inventory of those items. You can use a sticky note to write down which items you are bringing where. It will help you stay organized in both locations.

Now, if you have many people using different zones, it would be beneficial to label each zone and include a cleanup checklist for each area. This can be as simple as adding sticky notes to items or zones. Be mindful of all the people who use your office space so that you can keep up with the organizing habits you put in place.

Pro tip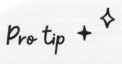

Keep your office space a place where you can feel motivated. Add in art pieces, quotes, or affirmations that make you feel inspired. You can also get some plants to add freshness to the room.

Organize Like a Pro

Tidy up your office using this list.

- Ask yourself: What is the purpose of this room?
- Make a list of all the things you are keeping.
- Group like things together.
- Create zones for each of those groups of items.
- Block off areas of your office space for each zone.
- Maximize your space by rearranging furniture or adding shelving or storage space.
- Put items back into the proper zones.
- Remove anything that doesn't fit into the zones you've created.

CHAPTER 13

Bathrooms

In my house, we have four bathrooms and they all have different purposes. Now I am sure you are asking, "How can a bathroom have different purposes?" Well, we have a half bath in our basement that is only used when people are in the basement. We have a half bath on our main floor that is used constantly during the day. Then we have a bathroom in our bedroom that my husband and I use to get ready. And we have a full bathroom that is for the kids.

Now why did I share all this with you? Because we are going to talk about organizing bathrooms and I want you to see how our bathrooms serve different purposes. This will help you start figuring out what purposes your bathrooms serve in your home.

FINDING ITS PURPOSE

To figure out what the purpose of the bathroom is, look at how it is used. This will help you decide what to store in that bathroom. Ask yourself these questions:

- Who is using the bathroom?
- How do you and your family use the bathroom?
- Are there any other locations that you and your family use to get ready, such as a vanity in the bedroom or a full-length mirror in another room?

I had a client who was drowning in toiletries. Each toiletry had to be stored in each of the bathrooms (one for the children and one for the parents), so she was buying multiples of everything. The sheer number of items started to take over these spaces. That's when I was called in. I looked at the bathroom situation and asked the questions I always do to get an idea of how the space is used.

Then we created a plan where the daughter and the mother used one bathroom and the son and the father used another. This way, they never had to buy multiple products because they could all be stored in the bathroom that person was using. Sometimes thinking outside the box can help you rework your space.

CREATING ORDER

Once you figure out the purpose of each bathroom, you can create order in that space. And by order, I mean ways you can get the things you need when you need them.

I had a client who had tons of storage in a powder room on the main floor. She started putting all the extra items in that bathroom and everyone in the family knew to look in that bathroom before saying they were out of the item. I love this idea, because not everything has to be crammed into a small space. You can and should only store items you use in your bathroom. Everything else can be stored elsewhere or not even brought into the house. This client also realized that she was holding on to things in her bathroom that she didn't even use or need.

As we were tackling her primary bathroom, we pulled out items from under her sink—expired medicines, sample face creams, and hotel travel bottles. She had to toss the things she was never going to use and find a storage solution for the other items.

Pro tip ✦ ◇

Remove your clutter first, then take advantage of your space.

To maintain order in your bathroom, start by getting everything out of the bathroom. This is one of those projects that really does require you to remove everything. If you are overwhelmed, just do under the sinks first. Then do the drawers. Then the cabinets. Keep an inventory as you go and get rid of things you don't use.

If you don't remember when you bought that mascara tube, throw it away. Makeup does have an expiration date. Those travel containers? Wash them out to use again. Sample packets should be used or discarded. Unopened items that you don't use can be donated to shelters or local organizations. Then you can put things back that you use all the time. Put those items in a location where you can get to them easily. Store extra items or overflow items together in one location so you can find them.

The remaining items? My guess is you can part with them, unless they belong somewhere else in your home. Then put those remaining items where they belong. Try to limit what you keep so you use what you have instead of collecting more things.

BATHROOM QUICK DECLUTTER LIST

This is a recommended list for the shelf life of common bathroom items and how long the product's ingredients stay active. Check the specific product's website for more details.

- Mascara: three to six months
- Eye liner: six months
- Creamy makeup: six months
- Sunscreen: one year
- Nail polish: two years
- Lotions: three years unopened and one year opened
- Shampoos and conditioners: three years unopened and one year opened
- Face washes: six months

TOWELS

How many towels do you have in your home right now? I have found that most people have too many towels, and those towels are taking up space that can be used for other things. One client had eighteen beach towels, twenty-four bath towels, thirty-two hand towels, and far too many face towels. There were only four people in her family and all of her extended family lived nearby. There weren't a lot of extra people coming to the house. We knew that we had to pare down her towel collection. We ended up giving each person in the house two towels, and saved two extra towels in case guests needed them. By donating the towels to a local animal shelter, we were able to clear some much-needed space in her bathroom and help animals in need at the same time.

You can do the same! I encourage you to try two towels per person in your house. You can keep two to four towels for guests. If you have a pool or go to the beach often, you may want a few more towels for that as well.

Organize Like a Pro

Use this list to declutter your bathroom(s).

- Get clear on the purpose of your bathroom(s).
- Take inventory of everything in your bathroom.
- Remove your clutter first, then stock your space.
- Check the shelf life of bathroom items (see recommended list in previous column).
- Put items that you use often back into the bathroom.
- Place your items where you can easily find them.
- Store extra items together so you can also find them easily.
- Limit the number of towels in your home.
- Donate unopened items to local shelters or organizations.
- Donate old towels to animal shelters.

CHAPTER 14

Kids' Rooms

When it comes to organizing kids' bedrooms, there are a few things I always do. I start by getting the kids involved when they are over the age of three. Yes, three-year-olds can totally help organize. In fact, it is a skill they should learn and learn early. It will save you so much time in the long run if the kids can keep their rooms tidy-ish.

Don't worry about the kids completely destroying the room as you organize. I have had a lot of clients share this with me, and I am here to tell you that when the kids are actually involved, things won't get destroyed.

Want to know why? Because they are going to be the ones in control of where to put things! Seriously! When you have the kids help you put things away in their room, they won't be "pulling out" all the

things because they are seeing what is going in the drawer as you put it in. This trick works wonders for younger children because they are more inclined to pull things out to explore what is inside the drawer. Try doing the opposite and have them put things in! You will be surprised by their excitement.

Now with kids' bedrooms, there are a few topics we need to cover. First, clothes. With children, they outgrow clothing quickly. Top that off with hand-me-downs and you could have a recipe for disaster in the clothes category. Another topic is toys in the bedroom. We will also cover books and keepsakes. When kids find an item they love, or something they have worked hard on, we need a way to let them keep it in their room but in an orderly fashion.

CLOTHES

Kids' clothes can be tricky. I have found that keeping specific types of items together helps kids find independence in selecting what they want to wear. So, group T-shirts with T-shirts. I try to store them in one drawer, but if there isn't enough room, then I use drawer dividers to keep the clothes sections separate. This visual helps kids see what goes where so they can actually take some responsibility for putting away their own clothes.

Also add labels to the drawers so kids can see what goes where. If you are up for it, I recommend file-folding clothes in the drawer (see page 26) so kids can see what they have. I have actually found it super helpful because my daughter and son can file-fold better than they can regular, stacking fold. It's weird, but it's true!

Kids outgrow clothes so fast, so it can be tough to keep up. I have a few ideas to help you. Have a bag or bin for outgrown clothes. Keep the lid off so you can just dump the clothes into that bin if they don't fit. I have a sticky note on the bin that lists the sizes and whether I need to wash any of the clothes. This just helps me stay on track for what is dirty and what isn't.

Have the bag or bin low for older children so they can take responsibility for their clothes. My daughter can be rather particular with her clothes, so if there is something she no longer likes, she just puts it in the bag and I don't have to worry about it. See, teaching them young pays off!

ORGANIZING OUTGROWN CLOTHING CHECKLIST

- Keep a bag or bin for outgrown clothes in the closet.
- Teach kids where to put clothing they no longer like into the bag or bin.
- Use sticky notes to keep the bin or bag organized with sizes of clothing.

TOYS

Another thing I do to keep kids' bedrooms organized is to limit the toy clutter. Some families have to keep toys in the kids' bedrooms because of space. My suggestion is to try to keep one or two types of toys in the bedroom, because the more toys you have in the bedroom, the more stuff there is to get cluttered. When there is more stuff to clutter the space, the less likely the child is to get a good night's sleep.

Pro tip

Create toy categories. For example, doll stuff is one toy category, cars and trucks is another.

When the kids have only a few categories of toys in their rooms, there is no need for piles to build up. Everything can either be displayed on shelves or put away in a bin. Keep it simple and your kids' rooms will stay tidy. See chapter 15 for more on how to limit toy clutter throughout your home.

TOY DECLUTTER CHECKLIST

- Try to keep few toys in the child's bedroom.
- Store a maximum of one or two toy categories in the child's bedroom.
- If limited on space, reduce all of the toys in the bedroom.
- Give everything a specific spot to go.
- Make cleanup easy.

BOOKS

I am a former teacher, so I am a huge lover of books. I had a giant book collection when my kids were born, and our collection of books has just kept growing over the years. While I would love to transform a room into a library, that is just not possible in our current home. So, we have to keep our books in check. If this is also true for you, then a great way to keep them organized is to only keep books you enjoy reading or looking at. You can sell the books you are finished with to a used bookstore and get credit to purchase new books. This is the best and more environmentally friendly way of book collecting!

Both of my kids' rooms have bookshelves where they can keep books. When they are done with a book, we add it to a book bin that we will then donate. I also have bins where I have stored books they aren't ready for yet.

I am a huge believer in having all the books in the kids' rooms, so I have designed their rooms to have lots of shelving space. However, this may be really overwhelming for your child as they struggle to find the book they want to read. To help with that, you can group books by category.

For my daughter, we have grouped all of her hardcover books together. Her paperback books are grouped together. Her chapter books are grouped together. Then her beginning reader books are grouped together. Organizing the books in this way makes things less overwhelming when my daughter looks for a book to read. This system also works for my son too.

You can also create a library in another location of your house, if you don't have enough room in the bedroom for books. Your kids could get a bin and pick books from this library to bring to their rooms. They could swap out the books each week to help limit extra clutter if the space doesn't allow for shelves to hold books. To create a library, collect all the books and store them in one location, typically the living room or basement where you can have a lot of bookshelves. Each child gets a bin to hold the books they are reading for the day or week. Then the child can swap out books from their book bin whenever they like.

This second option works best if your kids share a room, or you have limited space in the room. Also, this works if you have kids close in age or reading similar books, so you don't have to buy multiple copies of the same book, or if your child gets overwhelmed with the number of books in front of them. This typically happens if the child has a hard time focusing or has high anxiety. So, giving your child a bin of books to select from will support decision making and limit overwhelm.

Pro tip

Have beginning readers collect books they feel confident in reading independently in a bin. This will allow them to pull books out they can read and feel confident without pulling out all of their books from their bookshelf.

Pro tip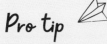

If you have a long bookshelf, use bookends to keep the books separated by category.

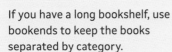

The third method to store books in your home is to have books throughout the house. This truly encourages kids to read. Keep sturdy bins or baskets and put books inside. Swap the bins around the house so the kids never get bored reading the same books in the same rooms.

Organize Like a Pro

Teaching kids how to pick up their rooms is a great organizing habit to instill in them. This list includes ideas for you and your kids. Teach your kids how to:

- Fold their own laundry.
- Put away clothing.
- Clean up their bedroom every night.
- Make their bed every day.
- Create a place for books to be stored.
- Remove clothing that no longer fits them.
- Limit toys in their bedroom.
- Give every toy category a specific spot in the bedroom.

CHAPTER 15

Toys

Toy clutter is a real thing. As parents, we feel guilty for not giving our kids what they want or what their friends have because we know that feeling of being left out. Or we feel that giving our kids gifts will make us feel less guilty when we have to work or be away from them.

The reason I suggest waiting until now to tackle toy clutter is because you have already seen what stuff you have that you have purchased out of guilt. Or maybe for sentimental purposes. Or because you may need it one day. Whatever the reason, you will see you are doing it with your kids' stuff too. So, we are going to discuss why kids don't need that many toys. Then we are going to learn ways to minimize

those toys. And we are going to chat about how we can keep the toy clutter at bay.

This is a big topic, so there is going to be a lot of work on your end to get yourself to a place of "favorite toys." When I say "favorite toys," I mean toys the kids actually play with, not the ones they claim they love. You know what I am talking about—the toys that they think they love because they just laid eyes on it, but you know that isn't the case. You know that toy hasn't been played with in a few months.

Why do kids think they need that toy? Because they can't differentiate between toys they enjoy and things they want. As adults, we know that there are things we enjoy, things we need, and things we want. The difference is we are able to rationally look at the pros and cons of purchasing each type of item. Kids are still learning the difference between wants and needs, which is why clearing the toy clutter and keeping it clear is going to be huge for them to understand the difference. Now, don't get me wrong, I love a good splurge every now and again. But don't make the splurge the norm.

Pro tip

When you do splurge for a toy, make sure there is a reason behind it. This will help limit the toy clutter because you have specific reasons for why you are investing in a quality toy.

WHY KIDS DON'T NEED ALL THE TOYS

So why don't kids need all the toys? Well, there is tons of research that says kids who have less stimuli (toys) are actually more creative and innovative than kids with tons of stimuli.

Ever notice that when your child has too many options they shut down? This isn't a coincidence. It is because they aren't able to figure out what to do.

When my kids have too many choices, they tell me they are bored. This is a signal to me that I have to limit the items surrounding them so they can make informed decisions and feel creative again.

The more toys the kids have, the less focused they'll be. During early years, children have short attention spans, which is only made worse when they are given tons of toys. A study published in *Infant Behavior and Development* found that when children are in an environment with fewer toys, they have a happier, healthier playtime. Researchers tested thirty-six toddlers for thirty minutes in two different playrooms: the first had four toys and the second had sixteen toys. Researchers found that when the toddlers were in the room with fewer toys, they were actively engaged for a longer period of time.

In another study, researchers reduced toys, activities, and excessive stimuli for children with attention deficit disorder (ADD). Within four short months, 68 percent went from being "clinically dysfunctional" to "clinically functional." The children also displayed a 37 percent increase in academic and cognitive aptitude, an effect not seen with commonly prescribed drugs like Ritalin. Again, this supports the fact that kids need less stuff!

Two German public health workers conducted an experiment called "Der Spielzeugfreie Kindergarten" (the nursery without toys), where they had a kindergarten classroom remove all of their toys for three months. The researchers found that after a few days of "boredom" the kids ended up creating games and found effective communication strategies. When they brought toys back, they had a discussion with the kids about which toys they wanted back, and the kids only wanted a few types of toys back in the classroom. Once toys were back, kids would create "more vivid drawings compared to before the toy removal project." Kids communicated better with each other, which is another validating point that kids don't need as much stuff as we think they do.

* HOW TO MINIMIZE *
KIDS' TOYS

To minimize the number of toys you have, start with an end in mind. Make a commitment to yourself and your family that, together, you will bring in fewer toys. And if you do need a variety of toys, you will create a plan to swap out toys so that the kids are not overstimulated with too many options.

First, envision what "done" looks like. Then work backward to get you through all the steps you need to complete that task. It seems really counterintuitive to think this way, but this is actually how our brains processes information.

Let's try with making our bed. Picture your bed completely made. So how do you get to that picture? First you have to put the pillows in place. Then pull the sheets up. Then the comforter or quilt. Then fold all that over and place the throw pillows on the bed.

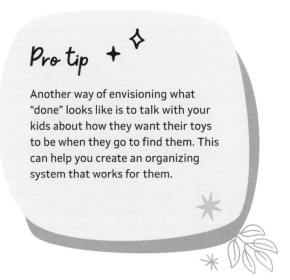

Pro tip ✦ ◇

Another way of envisioning what "done" looks like is to talk with your kids about how they want their toys to be when they go to find them. This can help you create an organizing system that works for them.

For my kids, they wanted their completed Lego creations out and all their Lego bricks color coded. They wanted all the doll stuff separate from the superhero stuff. This helped me figure out how we could store their things in a way they wanted to play.

Sometimes having actual pictures of the completed task can help as well. Let's say the kids want things stored in a certain way but you can't conceptualize how to get there. So, finding pictures of what done looks like will help everyone create a plan for how to get there.

Now that you have an idea of what done looks like, it is time to minimize the clutter. The most effective way to do this is to give everything a home or a spot. I have found that this is the best way to determine what to keep and what to get rid of.

Because you have the end in mind, you are able to get a good look at which toys the kids truly want to keep. In their vision of done, you should try to get really specific with where they want things to go. This is the best way to figure out what the kids' actual favorites are.

The storage bin of extra toys is also a good idea if you are unsure whether an item is a favorite. If you are unsure, put that item in a bin in your storage area. Then set a reminder on your phone for one month from the date. If they haven't used it within that month, it probably isn't worth saving, unless it is seasonal.

By watching what the child is playing with, you will quickly realize that not all the toys are their favorites. You are focusing on what the child is interested in. Maybe it is the color of the cars or maybe it is one particular doll. Whatever it may be, slowly remove the items that aren't being played with at all. You might find that there are some toys that get played with one day and don't the next. Those are the "filler" toys. Keep those toys as well as their favorites.

I want to note that if your child has a friend come over and the friend plays with all your kid's toys, that does not mean you should keep them. Kids enjoy seeing new things and trying out new items. And just because that friend doesn't have a particular item doesn't mean you need to keep it if your children aren't playing with it.

You may want to keep an extra doll in case a friend comes over, so keep a "filler" doll, but you don't need to keep eighty dolls just in case a friend comes over. And yes, I have had this conversation with clients and they all agreed once we parted ways with the bajillion dolls that their kids' friends didn't even notice.

Pro tip ☀

Another easy way to figure out their favorites is to watch your kids play with their toys for a week or so. Write down all the toys they are actually playing with. See whether they are digging in bins to find one specific toy. Start removing the toys that are still in the bin and placing them in a storage area in case your child asks for it.

SETTING EXPECTATIONS WITH TOYS

To keep the clutter at bay, start setting expectations for what "clean" looks like, how long things can stay out, and what happens if your child finds a broken toy or a toy gets put back where it doesn't belong.

Pro tip

Set expectations for what the kids are supposed to do with broken toys. Where do those broken toys go so they aren't in a bin with the toys that aren't broken?

To set expectations for your kids' toys, go back to how you set up the space. Get an idea of what done looks like. Then use that visual as a reminder for what is expected of the kids to keep toys organized. For example, are all the toys supposed to be put away in their bins every night? Every week? Never? Whatever you decide, set that expectation by writing it down. Use it as a "playroom rule" and hold the kids accountable for this expectation.

Create checklists or visual supports (that is just a fancy word for pictures and typically used for younger children or kiddos who may need more support to focus on the task at hand) to help children understand these expectations and know exactly what they have to do. This is where the follow-through comes into play. You need to hold them accountable for these expectations.

To create a checklist for the playroom, start with writing down all the things you want the kids to do in that room. Just get everything out on one piece of paper. I try to do this as we are cleaning up, so I get an idea of what needs to be done every night and every week. After you have everything written down, look at what should happen every day and circle those tasks. Think about whether you want those tasks done in a certain order as well.

Look at the list and see whether there is any task that can be done weekly. Maybe you have a task like sorting Lego bricks that only needs to happen once a week. Those can be on the weekly checklist.

I highly suggest laminating the checklist and using a dry erase marker to check off the tasks each day. I put our daily and weekly checklists back-to-back and laminated them together. That way we can hang the laminated checklist near the toys. And both checklists are together, making it easy for us to do our weekly cleanup when the time comes.

Using a checklist will give kids a sense of accomplishment when they get to check things off of their checklist! It is the exact same feeling you get from crossing off a task on your to-do list!

DECLUTTER CHECKLIST FOR KIDS

Write down all the tasks your child needs to do.

○ Circle tasks that need to be done daily.

○ Make a list of every daily task you want the child to do.

○ Laminate the list.

○ Teach your child how to check off a box with a dry erase marker when they complete a task.

To create a visual support, start by writing down a list of all the things you want the kids to do with the toys. Do they need to go somewhere specific? Is there a specific process for putting things away? Does everything have a designated bin? Once you have that list, see whether there is a process for putting the toys away. Does it make sense to start with one type of toy because that type of toy is always played with? Next, take pictures of those steps. Put those pictures in a sequential order so kids can follow the pictures to clean up.

One thing I did when my kids were younger was have a laminated piece of paper with four pieces of Velcro on it. Then I had pictures of all the toy bins we had. I put the pictures of the four types of toys that were out on the paper. Then the kids had to put away each toy that went along with each picture.

Let's say the kids played with cars and trucks, blocks, dress-up items, and stuffed animals. I would take out the pictures that went along with each of those types of toys. I would put the pictures on the laminated paper. The kids would each pick one of the pictures and find those toys to put away in the bin with the matching picture. Then they would put away the picture of the toys they were responsible for. Once those toys were put away, they would get to pick another picture of the toys to put away. By using pictures to help guide them, kids are able to see what goes with what type of toy, and it helps keep them focused on what they are supposed to be doing.

LABELING TOYS

To get kids to put things back where they belong, label everything. You can never over-label anything. Seriously, there is no such thing as over-labeling. There is only under-labeling and that is when you don't have enough labels so things get messy.

VISUAL SUPPORT CHECKLIST

- Write down the process you want the kids to do when cleaning up toys.

- Take pictures of the process.

- Turn those pictures into a visual support by using paper and arrows to show the steps.

- Add Velcro to the items so the child can move them as they complete the task.

The labels are going to help the entire family stay organized. When everything has a label and everything has a place, guess what? Everything will go back where it belongs. There is no excuse, and there is no thinking about where something goes. It simply goes back where it says. The best way to label toys is however the children can "read" them. That may be pictures or actual words (see chapter 8 on how to label toys).

Pro tip

No time to label? No worries! You can find picture labels online and print them off quickly. Then you don't have to worry about taking pictures yourself. Use what is already out there.

you actually take a step back and look at why you are buying toys, you will see why there is toy clutter.

If a family member is the one buying all the toys, then it may be time to have a conversation with them about types of toys to buy. One thing you can suggest is to have more "experiences" with family members, such as outings, classes, or activities.

When it comes to purchasing toys, choose quality over quantity. Select toys for quality and purpose rather than the actual amount of a particular type of toy. My son was really into trains. He would play with them morning, noon, and night. But we only had one set that would make an oval track with a bridge. He loved it. But my husband thought we needed more tracks and more trains. He thought that if the oval was all we had, our son would get bored and not want to play with his trains anymore. I refused to let any more tracks in the house.

Then, one day I put the tracks on the ground and my son created an epic track with his own bridges using Magna-Tiles and blocks that took him hours to build. When my husband saw it, he realized that more is not better. It would have completely stifled our son's creativity in constructing this train track. So, stop focusing on the amount and start focusing on the quality.

REDUCING TOY CLUTTER

The key to maintaining toy clutter is to live with minimal toys. Not "no toys," but fewer toys than you feel like the kids need. Start getting rid of toys that your kids aren't playing with and removing the sentimental value you have placed on that toy. Money is already spent on that toy, so there is no use holding on to it because "you spent good money on it." If no one is playing with it, get it out of your home because it is actually a distraction from the toys they do want to play with.

Another way to rein in toy clutter is to think about why you buy a toy before you actually purchase it. Most children don't buy toys for themselves; somebody else does. A healthy look at your own motivations may go a long way in solving this problem.

If you are buying toys out of guilt, really look at why you feel guilty. Is it because you are working long hours? Or you only see your child a few days out of the week? Make a conscious decision to choose time over stuff with your children. When

Pro tip

Declutter often. Make some clean sweeps on toys frequently. Have a designated area where you can put gently used toys and dump the broken toys or those with missing parts. Teach kids to do this as well. This may be one of the weekly items on your checklist. Each week declutter toys that can be donated, discarded, or sold.

Teach your kids how to declutter and get them involved in the decluttering process. Ask them what toys they like and what they don't play with. You can also use the one-in, one-out rule. When they get a new toy, an old toy is donated.

As they get used to this, they are more likely to part with toys quickly when they notice they aren't playing with them and that specific toys keep getting in the way of the toys they do want to play with. Use verbal reinforcement when you notice them decluttering without you reminding them. They need to know that it is okay to part with toys they don't use.

Pro tip

Turn decluttering toys into a game! Have your kids pick up five of their favorite toys and put them in the basket. Maybe they can only pick up the toys with their feet or elbows. You can quickly see which toys they run toward so you can use that to declutter other toys.

This next tip for reducing toy clutter can be a hot topic. Don't buy into fads. Those toy companies know how to make a toy a "fad." Don't fall for it! Kids only know about these fads because of other kids or television. Try to reduce television time and limit YouTube channels that promote those fad toys. Remember that toy companies actively market to kids. Try audiobooks or story apps so your kids use their imaginations to visualize a story.

When it comes to impulse buying, I have found that it typically happens when you are at a store and a temper tantrum is starting. Avoid temper tantrums in stores by setting expectations. Start by creating a plan when you go into a store. I give my kids specific items they have to remember to grab and put in the cart. For example, I will give my daughter the job to remember the apples and milk at the grocery store. She gets to put them in the cart and on the counter at the register. This helps limit her wanting to buy something because she feels like she already is buying something.

Finally, limit your own toys. Kids always learn more from examples than from words. If your life is caught up in always needing to own the latest fashion, technology, or product on the market, theirs will be too. It would be unreasonable to expect anything less from them. Really evaluate your items. You can also discuss budgeting with your kids. Teach them how to save their money for items they really want. This will also help them evaluate whether something is worth the cost so they can feel confident in their budgeting skills later on.

Another easy way to reduce toy clutter is to set a specific, physical space for one particular toy category. Depending on how your home is set up, having an actual playroom may not be possible, so you may have to store toys in different areas of your home. For example, place a play kitchen and play food in the actual kitchen. The art supplies can go on a cart to be pulled out of a closet or a corner of the room when needed. Blocks can go in a bin where there is a lot of floor space. Large toys like playhouses and ramps should all be grouped together in one specific area. When a bin gets full, declutter that bin to help keep toys to a minimum.

⟋★ TOY CATEGORIES ♥♥

I am a big believer in creating as well as limiting toy categories. I suggest keeping it to eight to ten categories tops. Too many categories can lead to overwhelm when kids want to play.

What is considered a category? Well, that is up to the types of toys your kids play with, but some suggestions might be cars and trucks are one category. Trains may be another. Art supplies could be its own category. Dolls may be a category, or you could break that up into types of dolls depending on how many you have and whether you want to limit them.

When you have more than one kid and they are different ages and have different interests, this is where you get to be super creative. One of my clients had three kids with vastly different interests. So, we kept the toys to ten categories but got creative with the types of categories. One of her kid's toy categories was things with wheels—cars, trucks, and trains. We got everything into one bin because that child was able to pick his favorites and keep them in the bin. Another category was called "building." This bin held blocks and tiles. The rest was donated. The last bin was for baby toys. It was an easy category to create because it was all the soft items that the baby could play with.

Younger siblings often want to play with their older siblings, but they may not be interested in the same toys. Don't feel the need to hold on to toys for a younger sibling if they really aren't interested. Watch what the kids are playing with, rather than what you think they want, and keep only what they enjoy.

TOY CATEGORIES

- Cars/trucks/things with wheels
- Action figures/Little People
- Trains
- Dolls
- Legos and blocks
- Games
- Art supplies
- Puzzles
- Dress-up items
- Dramatic play (play kitchen, tool bench)
- Music
- Sports equipment/balls

 STORING KIDS TOYS

Now this is the question of the hour—how do you actually store toys so kids will play? There isn't one answer. It really depends on the space and how your kids play, but I have some tips to help you get started.

Dolls

Storing doll accessories can be annoying, to say the least. I mean, you have the clothes, the tiny silverware, the shoes. Then there could be the giant play sets like a school or beauty parlor or gigantic dollhouse. How do you store them so the kids will actually play with them and not just have a place to contain the pieces they will never touch?

The first thing I recommend is getting the kids involved. Ask for ideas on how to organize their toys. You may be surprised by what they come up with. I typically say to store clothing together, store the food and plates together, and so on. If you have something that is breakable, store it in a Tupperware container.

Another thing I have done is to use pull-out drawers to hold different doll categories. One drawer can be for the actual dolls like Barbies. Another drawer can be for the clothes. Another could hold the food and plates.

By breaking up the types of doll toys, kids are able to find what they are looking for easier than dumping everything into a large bin. The giant play sets can be stored near the bins so they can play with ease. But they do take up a lot of floor space, so really decide whether these giant structures are worth it or whether you can find other things that don't take up the floor space but still allow children to play with their dolls in a similar fashion.

Pro tip

Find out how your kids play and use various items. Then organize them accordingly.

Dramatic Play Items

Dramatic play items are things like dress-up clothes and accessories used to play pretend. The easiest way to store them is in a tall bin without a lid. Simply put all the dress-up items in one bin and the accessories in another. The kids can dump them out, play, then shove them back into the bins. Easy peasey. This is probably my favorite way because it keeps it easy for everyone.

Pro tip

Store dramatic play items so they are easily accessible for kids. If they don't hang up their own clothes, why make them hang up their dress-up clothes?

Lego Bricks and Creations

I had a client who contacted me to help her organize her kids' Lego creations. Her kids enjoyed playing with the Lego creations they had made, so she wanted an organizing system for when the kids weren't playing with them. I knew we had to come up with a way to showcase her kids' creations. This also led to me doing similar things for future Lego builders as well. The organizing system we created included a lot of shelves and cabinets to store the bricks and creations. So, if you have a Lego builder, I strongly suggest creating shelving to store their completed pieces.

To store the bricks, I suggest looking at how your kids play with them. My kids wanted them color coded. But you or your kids may not want to keep up with the color-coding system. You simply have to go with what the kids want when they build. If they don't want color-coded bricks, then keep the Lego bricks stored in narrow bins to make it easy to find the pieces they want. If they do want the bricks color coded, make sure you have a bin specifically for "to sort." This will help if you don't have time to sort the bricks before you have to clean up. It can be a weekly checklist item!

Another way to do this is to divide them up by types and then store them in a bin based on the type of item they are. For example, you might put all the camping dramatic play items together. These are things like the pretend fire, sleeping accessories, and vests. All the construction worker items can go in another bin.

If you have the space for the second option and are okay with the upkeep, then do that. But if you are looking for a simple method, then the first option is better. Just remember to only keep the items your kids actually use and that fit them. When things get too small, it is time to get rid of them.

Oversized Play Pieces

Do you have oversized play pieces, such as extra-large cars and trucks, giant racetracks, or play structures? They can be really tough to store because they are so big and bulky. For the oversized cars and trucks, I create something I call the "parking lot." This is the space where all the cars and trucks get "parked." I like to store them under a table or bench.

The racetracks take up a lot of floor space, so I recommend storing those in an area where they can stay intact. We have used train tables to hold the racetracks, but you can still use them to play trains.

You can store the dollhouses and play structures on a deep shelf or bench, then take the structure down when the children want to play. This works well for younger children. For older children, it may be best to create something similar to the "parking lot." We call it a "village" and it is just a space on the floor where all the structures are stored, one next to the other. This helps limit the amount of floor space the items take up. If you are limited on floor space, try putting some of the large structures in your storage area and swapping them out every week to limit what is out on the floor.

Sports Items

My son loves playing knee hockey, basketball, and soccer in the basement. So, storing all the sports stuff was a top priority for me. I started by finding a tall storage bin that would hold all the items. There are carts that will work too if you have a lot of sports gear that needs to be wheeled outside. You can get really specific and group items by type, or you can just throw it all together in one bin, which is what we do.

I think storage options depend on how your kids play with the sports stuff. I had one client who was big into hockey. They also had two tiny basketball hoops in their basement, along with some other sports items. So, I had them store all the hockey items together in one bin and the rest of the sport stuff in another. This helped the kids play with their hockey stuff when they wanted, and the rest of the sports stuff fit perfectly into another bin.

Pro tip ♡

Let the kids decorate a piece of paper to use as a label for the parking lot or village. Hang it on the wall with painter's tape.

Board and Card Games

We are a big board game family, so we have a lot of them in our house. I have found that storing them can be tricky because not every box is the same size. I typically store card games in plastic picture holders. These holders help keep the cards together, but the kids can open and close the holders without ripping anything.

The board games do best when they are stored in their boxes stacked on top of each other. But that doesn't mean it actually works for keeping things contained within those boxes. Plus, the piles of boxes can end up with an even bigger pile of boxes if the game you want to play is at the bottom of the stack. So, to keep them organized, I recommend only stacking games three high.

Also, if the box can be opened on both sides, use packing tape to keep one side closed. When only one side can open, you don't risk losing pieces. I have used elastic headbands to hold boxes together too. That way, if you want to store your games on their side, you can keep the box closed without worrying about pieces falling out.

Pro tip

Does a game have a lot of small parts? Add a baggie to the inside of the box cover and add a strip of Velcro. This keeps the pieces from getting lost and holds all the parts together in one box.

Puzzles

When my kids were younger, we had a ton of wooden puzzles that didn't have a box or bag that they came in. So, I stacked them on a bookshelf. My kids would pull off the puzzles and every piece always ended up on the floor. I started to only leave out three puzzles because that was all that would fit on the shelf. And it worked. I would switch out the wooden puzzles each week. If you have the space to do that, I highly recommend trying it out for younger kiddos. If you don't have the space, try a puzzle organizer. They do help keep the puzzles together and give everything a space without the mess.

The biggest puzzles or bigger box puzzles are another storage dilemma that I had clients ask me about. One thing we do is tape the corners of the giant box puzzles so the box will stay together. I also use an elastic headband to hold the box shut. You can also use large zip-top bags to hold the puzzles. Then add a tag to the bag so you know what the puzzle looks like. Either tape a picture to the outside or cut out the cardboard image and store it inside the bag to show what puzzle is inside.

Stuffed Animals

Oh, the stuffed animals! I think my daughter is obsessed with stuffies because I was obsessed with stuffies when I was younger. I believe this is karma coming back to haunt me. So, I have had to learn quickly how to store stuffed animals, so they didn't take over her bed, her room, or my house!

You combat the stuffie hoard by keeping them in one large bin. Whatever doesn't fit doesn't stay. This visual helps my daughter and has helped my clients figure out which stuffed animals they truly love and which they don't.

Now this doesn't always work because your child may have a giant stuffed animal that doesn't fit in the bin. So, come up with an amount of giant stuffed animals that you are allowing to stay, then place them in a specific area within your home, such as on the couch in the basement, the bench in the playroom, or the chair in the bedroom. Wherever it may be, that is where it needs to go in order be considered put away.

Art Supplies

My kids are super crafty and love to make things. So, I have some tips for storing art supplies to keep things orderly. If you are able to, store your art supplies on a cart. This will help the kids wheel the cart to the table where they are creating their artwork, so art supplies don't end up on the floor.

Try to store art activities in zip-top bags, so you can see whether the craft or activity is completed. I've had some clients who had empty art activity boxes taking over their art rooms and they didn't even know it. Storing art items in baggies helps stop the collection of craft boxes.

The art materials like glue, scissors, pipe cleaners, and things used in multiple projects can be stored in zip-top bags as well. This way they are contained and won't scatter all over the floor. Or use an open container to hold those items if you are comfortable

with it. I like to store beads in an airtight container because if they get knocked over, they won't spill!

One of my favorite tricks for storing paper and coloring books is to use magazine holders. Most magazine holders will fit on standard-size shelves. The magazine holder is a great way for the kids to grab the paper they want without pulling out the entire stack. It also makes cleanup easier because you can slip paper into the magazine holder or put coloring books back into place.

Playdough and clay can be stored in bins with lids if you want to supervise when kids play with those items. The same goes for paints and other messy items.

Artwork and School Projects

Do you have piles of artwork sitting on your counter? I have had so many clients ask me what to do about kids' artwork and school projects. It isn't a one-size-fits-all solution. I know it isn't what you want to hear, but it is the reality of the artwork that piles up. I can't determine what you should keep and what you should trash. Only you can do that. But these tips might help!

Have the kids sort their artwork first. Create three piles. The first is to keep. The second is to take a picture. The third is to trash or recycle. (Just a side note that you have to find out what your city's recycling guidelines are before you throw something in there. For the purpose of this section of the book, I am going to say trash but that just means garbage or recycle based on what type of artwork it is.)

After your kids have gone through their artwork, you can do another sweep of the work. Sometimes I want to keep something the kids want to turn into a picture. Or vice versa. At first, I have more of a say than they do, but as you do this more, you will be able to follow their lead.

As you are going through their piles, ask yourself whether this piece of artwork is something you need to physically hold in order to appreciate. For instance, did your kid write a book? That is something I would keep because I would want to flip through the pages of it. The rest can be showcased in a photo book. This is a great way to determine quickly what to keep and what to trash.

After you have decided what to physically touch versus not, you need to make a game plan for the remaining items. The artwork you need to touch should go in the kids' memory boxes (see page 124). The rest needs to be sorted into a picture book or straight to trash. The straight to trash pile are those things like coloring pages or scribbles on paper that were filler activities. Ask yourself, if this were your artwork from when you were a child, would you want to look at it as an adult? Be honest because most of the time the answer is no. The only artwork I enjoy looking at from my past are bigger projects or picture books, not the random coloring page I did while I was waiting to pick up my sibling from school. Keep that in mind as you also make your pile for the picture book.

see page 124

Pro tip +

I love using photo book apps to create a book of my children's artwork. I create a folder with their artwork on my phone, then upload the images to one of the apps. It quickly turns it into a book my kids can look through whenever they want.

After you have selected the pieces of artwork to turn into a book, take pictures of each piece of artwork. Be really smart about all the work you want to put in this book. To take the best pictures of the artwork, place a piece of tagboard in front of a window or door. Try to get as much natural light as you can. Then lay the picture on the tagboard. Stand directly over the artwork and take a picture on your phone. Make sure you clean the phone camera before you take the picture, so you get a crisp shot. Continue to do this with each piece of artwork. Then save the pictures you took into a folder on your phone and create a book using the pictures you saved.

After you have taken the pictures, trash the artwork. You may have to show your child the pictures on your phone for them to be okay with you trashing their artwork. It is okay for your children to see this. They need to know that you have documented the work. Get the kids involved in creating their artwork photo book as well.

Find a schedule for taking pictures that works for you. For my family, we do it during winter break and once school ends. These are natural breaks that help us stop the paper pileup.

But where do you store those papers in between the photo shoots? I recommend having a specific spot where all papers can be collected. Maybe that is a magazine holder on the counter or a hanging folder in the playroom. Wherever it is, make sure you consistently have the kids put their papers there.

ARTWORK STORAGE CHECKLIST

- ○ Have kids sort through the piles first.
- ○ Sort into three categories: keep, photo, trash.
- ○ You do a second sweep to make sure every picture is in the proper category.
- ○ Store artwork in a child's memory box.
- ○ Trash all artwork that you are not keeping.
- ○ Turn remaining pictures into a photo book.

We've covered everything you need to know to tackle your toy clutter. This is where you have to get down and dirty to truly remove unwanted items from your home. Limit what you bring into your home and teach your kids how to do it as well.

RANDOM TOY CATEGORIES

Okay, so you have some leftover toy categories or only a small number of items that the kids play with that may not need a giant bin. What do you do with these types of toys?

My favorite way to store these is in a zip-top bag for smaller toys. It keeps the toys contained and can be easy for the child to grab and play with. I love creating a new bin for larger toys. Give that random category a home, even if the bin has to stay on the floor because there is no longer shelf space. I like to do this when the kids get a few new toys for the holidays or birthdays and they aren't totally sure whether they are going to play with the new toys. So, we keep them in a baggie or bin. As the kids play with their new toys, I try to figure out whether they love the toys or whether they are just getting in the way. Then we can either create a new organizing system for those toys or they can leave the toy area.

Organize Like a Pro

Use this list to start limiting toy clutter.

- ○ Make a goal to live with fewer toys.
- ○ Get kids to help with decluttering toys they don't play with.
- ○ Create toy categories.
- ○ Find storage bins that work for the toys you want to keep.
- ○ Store toy categories in areas that make sense for the kids when playing.
- ○ Look at the reason why you want to buy a toy.
- ○ If you are unsure about which toys the kids play with, put the toys in a storage area and wait to see if they ask for that toy.
- ○ Create a parking lot or village for oversized items.
- ○ If you have random toy categories, create a temporary storage spot to see whether the kids play with those toys.
- ○ Create a plan for dealing with kids' artwork.

CHAPTER 16

Paper Clutter

Paper clutter. It is probably my least favorite thing to organize because whenever we get through a pile of paper, it feels like we haven't even made a dent. You could easily spend an hour sorting through papers only to look up to see that there are still countless more piles to sort. It can be maddening!

The paper piles can easily accumulate if we don't stay ahead of ourselves to stop that from happening. According to the National Association of Productivity and Organizing Specialists (NAPO), it is estimated that about 80 percent of papers you keep in your home you never use or look at again. This means that you probably have way more paper stored in your filing cabinets than you actually need. So why are we holding on to so much paper?

The biggest thing I have heard from clients is that they feel like they have to hold on to the paper because they might need it again—things like notes from seminars, old books from college, business cards, old résumés. These are all things that we really do not need to keep, as it is just clutter.

I have to break it to you that odds are you won't need it again. And if you do, you can easily find that information in a quick Internet search.

I also want to remind you that most of your college books and notes are outdated. Not because you are old, but because new information is generated quickly. So, your old college notebook isn't going to help you succeed at the job you have right this second. Yes, I am being tough, but when it comes to paper, you have to be.

HOW TO TACKLE THE PAPER PILEUP

Deciding which types of paperwork you need—whether the physical documents or digital documents—is really a matter of personal preference on most items. My rule of thumb is anything that you signed, keep the original. Anything that has to do with taxes or contracts should be kept. But your notes from college? Trash. Those business cards? Put the contact in your phone and get rid of the paper. That bill you paid? Have you thought about making it an electronic bill that you can flag in your email?

The second reason we keep papers is for sentimental reasons. And that is okay! But just remember that sentimental paper is going to pile up quickly. Ask yourself whether you truly need something or not.

FIFTEEN TYPES OF DOCUMENTS YOU SHOULD KEEP

1. Contracts
2. Tax documents
3. Social Security cards
4. Birth certificates
5. Marriage certificates
6. Deeds
7. Appraisals
8. Power of attorney
9. Diplomas
10. Death certificates
11. Military discharge paperwork
12. Passports
13. Life insurance policies
14. Important health documents
15. Mortgage/rental agreements

HOW TO DECLUTTER THE PAPER YOU HAVE

The first thing is to turn as much of the papers as you can into digital files. You can search your computer for those documents easier than if you had the document stored in a filing cabinet.

Another way to declutter the paper is to set a timer. This gives you a specific amount of time to go through paper piles. Paper can easily be shoved into drawers and filing cabinets, taking up space. So, set a timer and make yourself go through the papers daily or weekly to reduce the clutter.

It's time to be realistic. You do not need to hold on to every piece of paper, so be mindful about what you keep. Ask yourself the questions on page 155 when dealing with paper clutter. As you go through your papers and documents, these questions will come in handy to help you decide whether a paper is really worth keeping.

Pro tip

You can find most manuals online. Download a digital copy and store it on your computer desktop to make it easy to find when you need to fix an appliance.

HOW TO STOP THE PAPER PILES FROM PILING UP

I feel that stopping the paper piles can almost be as daunting as decluttering the paper piles! Why? Because the paper never seems to go away! But we can stop a lot of paper pileup with little organizing habits we instill in ourselves.

One way to get paper to stop piling up is to deal with that mail right away. This means recycling the mail and shredding things immediately. Don't let them pile up on the counter. Try keeping a recycling can near your main entrance so you can toss any junk mail into it before it makes its way to your counter.

I have clients keep a shredding machine near their garage door so they can shred any documents that they do not need but don't want to just recycle. I love this idea because it is a great way to stop the paper clutter from piling up or collecting it to "shred later." Many of my clients have boxes full of papers they wanted to shred but their shredder broke, or they didn't have a shredder. The easy fix to that situation is to replace the broken shredder or find a shredding place to get those documents out of the house ASAP.

You can also contact the mailing companies that send you junk mail and request that they stop sending you mail. There is usually a number or website on the back of catalogs where you can request not to receive them anymore. You can contact the charities or organizations you donate money to and request they only send you emails for donations. This not only cuts down on your paper clutter, but also helps them save money by not sending stuff to you via mail!

Another trick is to create a home for the paper. Don't let it pile up and then "deal with it later." Create an organizing habit first. Let's say that your paper ends up on the kitchen counter. Instead of letting it just take over the entire counter, give the paper a designated space like a tray or magazine holder. This will help support everyone in the family because they know exactly where the paper should go.

Paper in the office can be contained by using box file folders or magazine holders. Keep it near your computer so you can easily grab the papers you want and neatly file the ones you don't need at the moment. This system helps you really think about keeping and storing less paper because you don't have as much space to store it all.

Organize Like a Pro

Use this list to help you declutter and maintain an organizing habit for your paper.

- Take action by getting clear on what organized paper looks like to you.
- If you need, buy a shredding machine. Or find a local business that will shred documents for you. Add shredding dates to your calendar with a reminder, so you never miss a drop-off.
- Move a recycling bin near where your mailbox or main entrance is.
- Set up a drop zone to collect papers.
- Turn as many items into digital form as possible.
- Only keep important documents in your filing cabinet (see page 113).

CHAPTER 17

Holiday Decor

One topic that I feel is never covered in organizing books is holiday decor items. I feel that most people talk about day-to-day organizing instead of the things that might take up more space in your home if not decluttered and handled with care.

Holiday decor are the items you use for the holidays, such as Christmas, Valentine's Day, Hanukkah, Kwanza, or religious items that are not always on display. These items can take up a lot of space in your home or in a storage facility that you are paying for. If you enjoy all your holiday decor and can afford the storage for it, then go for it! But if you are looking to actually pare down the decor, then this chapter will help you.

DECLUTTER THE HOLIDAY DECOR

What I have learned over the years about decluttering holiday decor is that most people have a hard time letting go of pieces because there is sentimental attachment to them. Maybe an ornament was from when you were a child. Or a statue or platter was given as a gift when you got married. While these gifts are incredibly thoughtful, they may not always fit with our own style.

I have a story for you regarding the gifting. My mom bought us a bright orange pumpkin candle for Halloween one year. I didn't have any Halloween decor, so I put it out on our mantel. The following year, I ended up getting some items to decorate, but the candle my mom gave us didn't really go with the other colors I was using. I left it in our Halloween decor box thinking I would use it the following year.

Well, each year I never used the candle because the other decor I was using didn't match with the bright orange candle. I had to part with it because it wasn't doing anyone any good sitting in a box being brought upstairs for Halloween only to be brought back to the basement a few days later.

Letting go of the unwanted holiday decor does not mean you aren't grateful for the gift. You need to take that mind-set out of the equation. Holding on to something that you aren't using isn't helping the person who gave you the gift either.

What I have found to be the easiest way to part with holiday decor you haven't used is to declutter before putting the holiday decorations back into their storage bins when the holiday is over. The reason why I like doing this is because you may be already sick of the decorations since they have been up for so long. You are ready for a change, so you are more likely to part with items you may not have been able to if you decluttered before the holiday started.

After looking at your holiday decorations for so long, it is easy to see what you can part with. I know the sentimental pieces can be trickier. I have had clients make picture books of old ornaments that have broken.

One of my clients who was really into photography took all of her and her husband's ornaments from their childhoods and turned them into a book that they displayed every Christmas. Each one of the ornaments was on its own page in the book. She added garlands or elves or other Christmas decorations around the ornament when she took the picture. On the opposite page, she included a story or memory regarding that ornament. This book allowed her to part with broken ornaments that held a special sentiment, and it was more meaningful than holding on to a broken ornament that would never be displayed again.

I had another client turn all the broken ornaments into new ornaments. She found a company that takes broken glass and puts them into a clear ornament with etching on the new ornament. I thought this was a great way to showcase old ornaments and give them new life without holding on to broken pieces.

You can get creative with ways to remember your old holiday decor that has sentimental value. Obviously, I am a fan of creating picture books because you can get really good-quality books and use them as decor on your coffee table during the holiday season.

There is nothing worse than having bins of holiday decor with nothing you want to display. Stop holding on to the items that do not work with your decor just because someone gave it to you. It will help you have more room for more decorations that you actually enjoy and want to display.

Now if you don't use something this one holiday season but may use it the next, add a sticky note to remind yourself that if you don't use it the next holiday season, you can part with it. I find the sticky note reminder helpful. When you open the bin to start decorating for the next season, you may have forgotten what you used and what you didn't. The sticky note is your reminder that you didn't use something. When you look at it again, a year later, you may find that your attachment to that item has changed. And you may be more likely to part with it before the holiday because of the note you left yourself.

STORING

Once you have decided what to keep and what to declutter, you can store the items. Now I am sure you are asking yourself, "Why we are talking about storing?" Don't you just throw the holiday decorations in a bin and call it a day? Sorry to say, no you don't!

When you store the holiday decorations in a way that is easy to unpack, you are not going to have as many (if any) broken or misplaced items. How many times have you been decorating for the holidays and wanting to use a particular decor piece but you can't find it so you spend a lot of time searching for that item when you could have just been decorating and enjoying yourself?

To store the items, I suggest bins with labels for each holiday. Then take inventory of each bin as you pack it up at the end of each holiday season. Get a piece of paper and write down which items are going into which bin. You can be super specific or just general. When I do this, I am more general. I say "all stuffed pumpkins" instead of labeling each pumpkin that I am putting in the bin.

Tape the inventory to the front of the bin. My bins are clear, so I put the inventory list on the inside of the bin with the words facing out and taped to the inside of the bin. That way I can see what is in each bin. I also have a giant label with the holiday on each bin.

Try to keep similar decor pieces together. Try storing all items that go on your mantel together. Maybe you can store tree trimming together with the tree stand or the covering if it will fit. Love decorating your banisters? Put all those items together in a bin. Have holiday plates, platters, and cooking utensils you only use for that holiday? Store those items in their own container. When it is time to decorate the following year, you can unpack and decorate quickly.

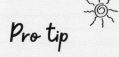

Pro tip

Try storing items together based on how you decorate for the holiday season. This will make decorating the following year much easier and less time-consuming.

One client had me pack up her Christmas decor one year after Christmas season. A year later, I got an email from her saying that unpacking and decorating took her a few hours instead of a few days, simply because we grouped all the decorations together based on how she decorated her home. She was able to easily take the items out of the bin and display or hang ornaments. Then she was done.

Also, the inventory is really helpful if you decide to change how you are displaying the items. You can look on the inventory list you created to see what decor pieces you have in each bin so you can pull out those items easily, instead of dumping each bin out and hunting for what you need.

FIVE THINGS YOU CAN DO NOW TO STORE HOLIDAY DECOR

1. Take inventory of items in each holiday decor box.

2. Declutter after the holiday is over.

3. Store items together based on how you decorate.

4. Keep holiday decor separate for each holiday you decorate for.

5. Store holiday serving platters, trays, and cookware together.

☆ NOT ALL DECOR 💗 IS CREATED EQUAL

You spent all this time decluttering your holiday decor and storing it so you can find it easily. But you are not going to *not* buy new decor. So how can you find pieces to add to your decor collection that are both meaningful and will last? That is where you have to evaluate the holiday decor's purpose. Why are you going to invest in that new holiday decor piece? Where is it going to go?

I know that after each holiday, stores have massive discounts on holiday items. And I enjoy shopping for holiday stuff the following year. But I always have a plan. I want you to try making a plan as well.

Before you run to the store, take inventory of what holiday items you have. The inventory list is really helpful for this! Then you can either take mental notes or real notes when you go into the store. You can shop for the deals and discounts with your inventory list, so you are not spending money on things you already have. You can find the holes or missing decor pieces that you would like for the following year. And you can feel confident about your purchasing decisions because you used the inventory list of what you have in your home.

If you part with a holiday decor piece because you didn't use it, make sure you are not just replacing that item with a similar item. I have seen that happen too. I have had clients spend hours decluttering their holiday decor only to replace the items they decluttered with basically the same things. If you feel this is you, then take inventory of what you decluttered. Bring that with you to the store so you don't purchase anything on that list. This will prevent buying unnecessary things and you won't have to constantly do big declutters of your holiday decor.

Pro tip

Don't like clear bins? Color code your holiday decor bins. Red can be for Christmas, orange for Halloween, etc.

Organize Like a Pro

Start organizing your holiday decor by using this list.

- Declutter holiday decor items after the holiday season has ended.
- Take out all the holiday decor items and only put back items you used that holiday season.
- Make an inventory list of items you have in each bin.
- Add that inventory list to your bin.
- Make a copy of that list if you are going to purchase new holiday decor pieces.
- Add sticky notes to items you didn't use this year but aren't ready to part with yet.
- Store all holiday items together.
- Group holiday items together based on how you decorate with them.
- Create a "do not buy" list of items you are decluttering, so you don't purchase similar items again.

CHAPTER 18

Cherished Items

Those special items you hold onto. You know. Your kids' outfits from when they came home from the hospital. Your photos when you were a child in those giant photo albums. The jerseys from your sports teams you played on when you were younger. They truly are important, but you don't need them on constant display.

The amount of stuff we want to keep because it seems "special" can easily pile up. So, I always ask what is the point of keeping all these things? The typical response is to remember it. Then I try to go deeper with the reason they want to keep these things. I ask if the child has had any say in what stays and what can go. I ask if they have similar stuff from when they were a child and if they enjoy looking at it. I ask if they are keeping it because they aren't sure whether it is something special.

You do not need to hold on to something that was special to someone else. You can say no to family members wanting to give you their sentimental items. Setting boundaries around what you want to keep will help you stop sentimental clutter from piling up.

Pictures can be stored in photo albums that you swap out each season. This keeps things new, but you are still able to see the pictures you enjoy.

It doesn't have to be difficult to deal with the items you cherish. You just have to get creative about what to keep and what can be donated/sold/trashed. I can't tell you what to do with those pieces that you are wondering about, but see page 124 for some questions you can ask yourself to help guide your decisions.

A lot of times, we hold on to things because we think they are special. Like a binder of activities the kids did in preschool. That giant binder can take up an entire bin. But what if you just keep the pictures that were inside and get rid of the binder?

These special or cherished items can easily consume your home. It can be tough to part with things. But I am here to say it is okay to part with them if you want to. Only keep things if you have the space to do it.

Pro tip

Keep cherished items by displaying your favorites without holding on to everything. You are keeping the pieces you love and showcasing them instead of hiding them in a box in the basement.

QUESTIONS TO ASK YOURSELF WHEN LOOKING AT SENTIMENTAL ITEMS

- Are you displaying this item? If not, why are you not displaying it in your home right now? If you are displaying that item and enjoy looking at it, then you don't have to worry about this question. But if it is an item in the basement that you only look at when you move things around, then why are you keeping it?

- Do you physically need to hold this item to appreciate it? What if you take a picture and create a book with stories in it rather than hold on to the physical item?

- Are you holding on to this item out of guilt? This is key when you are given things. You end up feeling guilty for not wanting that item. But what good is it if it is just sitting in your basement?

- And here is a tough love question: Do you want your kids to have to deal with that item once you are gone? I know this is really dark, but you have to think about it in these terms. In *The Gentle Art of Swedish Death Cleaning,* the philosophy is that you part with items so your family doesn't have to as you get older. If you are struggling with this topic, I highly recommend reading this book to guide you through the death cleaning and getting rid of things that your family will not want.

Once you answer all of the questions in the previous column, the decision to keep or let go of a cherished item will become much clearer. You already know what to do with the items you need to let go of, but what do you do with all those items you want to keep? You can create a memory box to keep your cherished items. I suggest creating a memory box for each family member. But just one memory box, not multiple boxes. I have seen clients create a baby box, a toddler box, a preschool box, an elementary school box, and so on!

CREATING A MEMORY BOX

To create a memory box for each family member, start by getting a large bin. Make sure it isn't too large that you can't store it anywhere. Grab a piece of paper and a pen. You will need it! Then take all those special items and dump them out. Make sure you can see everything because we are going to do a quick scan of each item. You might notice that your eyes go directly to the most important things. Your brain just knows. Trust it! Write down all the items you notice right away. These are items your brain registers as important.

After you write everything down, find those items. Pick them up and hold them. Then make a final decision whether they should go in the memory box or not. Sometimes when you hold an item you can physically feel your body's energy change. That energy change may feel like goosebumps or your shoulders make go back and your chest goes out. Or your shoulders slump over, and you start to feel small. All of these are energy changes in your body are reactions to physically touching an item and your body remembering that emotion.

Be really mindful about what you keep because you are realistically passing it down to your kids. And do they really need your letterman jacket from high school? (I am looking at my husband while writing this!)

Pro tip

If your memory box starts to pile up, it might be time to rethink what you're keeping. The reason I like using only one box is because it gives you a defined space to keep things. When you have a clearly defined space, you are more likely keep things inside that space. So, you are only allowed to keep all your memory items inside that one bin. I know you can do it, so try it!

Organize Like a Pro

Declutter your cherished items with this list to help you get started.

- Deal with sentimental items as they come into your life.
- Go through cherished items you have in your home right now.
- Listen to your body language and emotions to decide whether you want to keep an item.
- Create a memory box for each member of your family.
- Make sure that each member has a say as to what they want to keep in their memory box.
- Turn cherished items into memory books, scrapbooks, or photos instead of holding on to the physical items.
- Set boundaries around other people's cherished items.
- Do not take family items if you don't want them or will not use them.
- Ask yourself whether you want your children to deal with this item after you are gone.
- Create an organizing habit for all new cherished items.

CHAPTER 19

Bringing It All Together with Decoration

While I absolutely love organizing, I also absolutely love decorating. I really feel like the two go hand in hand. The reason is that when you have your home decorated to make you feel happy, then you want to keep the space looking like that. That means you will continue to keep the organization you have created.

When decorating, envision what you want to feel in the room. Do you want the space to feel cozy, inviting, warm, formal? Give yourself some words you want to feel when you are in that space. I like starting in the living or family room. Because you already gave that room a purpose, you can find decor you love that meets the purpose of the room.

Pro tip

Give each room an adjective for how you want to feel when you walk into it. Use that adjective as you decorate.

Look around the room. Look at the paint color on the walls. How does that color make you feel? Everyone has a different take on colors, so I am not going into depth about them. But I will say that if you feel a particular way about a color, then you have to go with that feeling instead of trying to make it happen.

My husband and I did a large kitchen renovation a few years ago, and we had to decide on a paint color for our kitchen. We had one entire wall of backsplash, so it ended up being only three walls that needed paint. There was one full wall, another wall with windows, and the third wall with doorways.

I struggled so much with color because I wasn't listening to myself. I was trying to find inspiration online rather than using my gut to help me. So, we ended up painting the kitchen this really light blue color that basically looked white. The kitchen felt unfinished and really sterile. It didn't feel cozy, homey, or inviting.

The rest of the house has bold colors and cozy feelings throughout. I wanted our kitchen to feel the same. But I just kept putting off the project. I was being very indecisive about it all.

A few years later—yes, years!—I was looking through paint colors for a different project and this dark green color just spoke to me. So, I asked my friend her opinion because she has a good eye for this

kind of stuff. She said the dark green color would be perfect. So, we painted the kitchen a dark green. I was nervous because it was so bold. But once it was up on the walls, it was the exact feeling I wanted in the kitchen. Paint can totally transform a room without buying any new stuff. So, let the paint color speak to you or hire a professional to pick a color. I promise it helps so much getting outside advice

You also want to look at your furniture. Are these pieces working for you? Just because you have something doesn't mean you are stuck using it if the furniture isn't working.

Pro tip

Change the paint color of your space first before adding decor pieces.

Sometimes just swapping out things or finding items that are better suited for the space will help you create order in your home. Start with giving everything a home or specific spot in that room. This will help you declutter the things you don't need. Give your rooms a purpose for how you want to use them (see the worksheet on page 148). Then you can start decorating. And when I say decorating, I am talking about making the room or space feel like yours, not someone else's.

Also, if you decide to paint or get new furniture, do that before you move on to the next step. You want to see the large things done first so the rest can fall into place.

SHOPPING YOUR HOME

I am very big on shopping your home. Now when I talk about shopping your home, I am talking about going around your entire house and collecting all the trinkets and items that you could decorate with and creating your own little store from those items. Shop your home before you buy any new decor so you can see what you already have first. You can shop at stores once you find out what items you need.

Pro tip

Involve the kids and make it an arts and crafts day! As you shop your home, let your kids pick out items you can repurpose and have them repaint or do creative things with those items.

I truly believe that shopping your home is the best way to decorate because you aren't buying things just to buy. And you can be really thoughtful about where and what you bring into your home. So, let's walk through how you actually do this "shopping your home" thing.

Maybe you are ready to tackle a room, but you aren't loving the decor. Let's use your family room as an example because it is the easiest to explain. Start by clearing everything off the mantel and shelves. Leave nothing on any surface. You want a total blank slate to do this process because when you have things already in place it can be difficult to envision how it would look in a different way. We get stuck in the same ideas if we don't have a clear space to see possibilities.

HOW TO SHOP YOUR HOME

○ Clear off everything in the space.

○ Clean the shelves, cabinets, etc.

○ Walk around your home and pick up items that could go in your space.

○ Display all the items so you can see what you have collected from around the house.

○ Start adding items to the shelves, cabinets, etc.

Once everything is off, clean each shelf and mantel. Those dust bunnies don't go with your newly organized home anymore! Also dust off the items that were on the shelves and mantels. They were probably dirty too, so give them a good cleaning.

Then walk around your house and pick up items you have that could go in that space. Do not worry if they are already in a spot. You might find they work better somewhere else. It is surprising how easy it is to see one item only be one type of decor when it could easily be transformed in a different space.

Collect all the things that could or may work in the room. I have even gone as far as collecting things that I know won't go there but I thought I would give it a try. Set those items up in another room or on a table so you can see everything together. You may notice that one or two pieces just don't go with the rest of the things, and you may be able to declutter before you decorate. And who doesn't love a good declutter before they decorate?

Now you are ready to start decorating you shelves, mantels, and spaces.

✶˙✧ DECORATING TIPS ⋙♡
☆ FROM AN ORGANIZER

I love decorating, but I have to say that I am not a designer. I did take one design class in college though. This section just includes things I have found helpful when decorating and organizing my home.

When you are setting up furniture, make sure there is a natural flow to the room. I like to think about how I would walk into a room and move in that room when deciding where to put furniture. Also, I like to think about having conversations with people and where the television will go because these are real things in real living spaces.

Pro tip ✦✧

Walk through a room like you would want your family to walk through it and then notice whether you are bumping into things or doorways are blocked. Then move furniture for a better flow.

While I love things looking pretty, they need to be functional. If you have a couch where no one can see the television and that is where you spend the majority of the time watching television, then why have the couch there? While Pinterest and Google are great resources, they aren't always the most realistic when it comes to designing a room for real people, not a photo. Keep that in mind when placing furniture.

Now when decorating shelves or mantels, I like to use the rule of three. When you place things in groups of three, the eye enjoys that grouping. Odd numbers are more appealing to the eye than even numbers. The goal is to group things that are pleasing to the eye.

Pro tip

I also like to play with height when grouping things together in threes. A tall item goes in the back, then something that is medium height, then something that is low. I like using vases or candle stands as my tall piece. I have also used mirrors, pictures, and lamps for tall items. Finding textured or colorful items helps break up basic pieces.

Now if you have a more mathematical or scientific brain, try setting up a shelf by using what is called the rule of thirds. That is when you divide up a space into nine equal squares. Visualize this grid when setting up a shelf. Start with a tall object and place it near one of the vertical lines in your imaginary grid. Let's say you have a picture. Center that on one of the vertical lines. Then place some greenery as your medium item on or near the other vertical line you have drawn in your head. Lastly, place something

small in the bottom middle of the grid. This mental image of a grid is a great way to design a space. You can see that it helps you create a lovely image in your head, and you are pleased to look at it.

You can also play with balance and have more things on one side of the imaginary grid, leaving more white space on the other side. Keep things together in odd numbers and your brain will thank you later.

Pro tip

Try picturing your space like a grid of three squares by three squares. Then decorate your space within those visuals.

You also want to think about color choices. Using the rule of three, you can have three main colors to keep a space looking cohesive. Ever notice that when you are in a room with too many colors, your brain gets overwhelmed? I know mine does. I like the rule of three when it comes to colors as well.

I like picking one main color and two supporting colors. For our living room, the main color is a deep purple, and the supporting colors are pink and yellow. I personally feel that gray, white, and black are neutrals, so they don't count in the rule of three approach to color combinations. I may be wrong, but that is just what I feel.

After I pick the colors, I try to keep as much of those colors in the pieces I use to decorate. That way I am not bringing in more stuff to look at. Instead, I am keeping it consistent. My eyes enjoy that, and I feel it makes the space cozy when you have three colors to look at instead of just one or two.

FILLING IN THE GAPS

Using the items you have from shopping your home, you can now start decorating. Do not link any item to where it was stored before. You want to use items that work in the space so you can change up how your home looks. It keeps things interesting.

Once I have created vignettes on my shelves that I like, I will look to see what I am missing. What are things I may need to find to fill in those gaps, to make the look complete?

I will go look at my holiday decor to see whether there is anything in those bins that works for my new decorating scheme. Sometimes I have been able to find things that work wonderfully that were stored with my holiday decor. If you can't find anything, make a list of things you feel would bring the space together. For me, I usually notice that I need greenery items to go inside vases or candles in the colors I am working with.

Pro tip

I change pillow covers if I don't want too many colors going on in the room at one time. I prefer pillow covers over pillows because the pillow covers are easier to store. You can just fold them up and put them in a bin in the basement rather than having to house all the pillows. You can change them out for holidays or new color schemes and store them with the seasonal decor.

I will make a list of the things I need to find that will finish the space. Then I go and put the items back or rearrange where items will go in different parts of the house. Because I shopped the house, I now get to redecorate all my rooms. It is a fun way to change things up without spending any money.

Most of the time, I don't have to get anything new. It may just be something to put in a vase or a wreath to add to a mirror. It's nothing major and most of the time I can DIY a project using things I have. That is why I suggest shopping your home first, then putting things back to give your home a new feel.

Make lists for ways you can fill in the gaps to finish your decor. Maybe you need paint to change out the color of a picture frame. Or you need to print off new pictures for your frames. Do it rather than just sit on it because once the room is organized and decorated you will feel incredible. Your space will feel like you. You will want to be hanging out in that room because it feels like home.

Start buying decor pieces that can go together with items in your home. For example, find similar colors or types of items that can work in many areas. Select versatile pieces that are not meant for only one room of your home. This way, you have pieces that go together and can be used in different rooms.

Try to define your decorating style. It does not have to be fancy or "the proper terms." Simply find words that you feel encompass your home. Think of the adjectives you used to describe the room and add that to your decor style. Maybe you are modern boho. Or colorful farmhouse. Or traditional chic. Or old-world charm. Whatever words you like to describe your home, go with it. Do not overthink it. It could change, but you need to start somewhere. Next, find items that you feel meet those words. This way, your decor items give your entire house the overall feeling of whatever decorating style you are going for.

Let me give you an example. I like a more farmhouse/hygge feel in our home. Not the cows on the wall farmhouse, but the cozy feeling of a farmhouse.

So, the decor I purchase fit into that style. This way, when I shop my house, all the pieces work in every room. I can use a vase and filler in our bedroom and then move it to the living room and it looks like it belongs there. You do this so you are not collecting too many pieces that are only meant for one area of the house. Now you can start decluttering things that don't feel like you or your home.

This method prevents you from holding on to items that do not serve you anymore and gives you options for future decor. You aren't stuck with one thing in one room only. Things can be more fluid in moving throughout your home. You can rearrange and redecorate as often as you want without worrying about buying new things. You can simply shop your home because *everything* in your house works *everywhere* in your home.

TIPS FOR MAKING THE SPACE FEEL COMPLETE

- After you decorate, take note of what feels off.
- See whether you can find something to make it feel complete.
- Make a list to use as reference while searching for new items.
- Don't just buy to buy. Find items that actually work with your space.
- Redecorate spaces that you took items from while shopping your home.

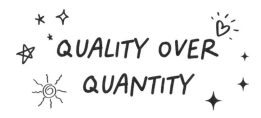

QUALITY OVER QUANTITY

One piece of advice that I have learned over the years is to invest in quality pieces. This is something I have learned the hard way. For the longest time I would buy cheap things to add as decor, but I would get sick of it or it would break quickly. I would end up buying more stuff because I needed to replace it. What I realized was that I was spending more money on cheap items than I would have if I bought quality pieces from the beginning.

When I first moved into my apartment in downtown Chicago, I bought cheap items that worked in my tiny apartment. Well, a year later, I had to move into a different apartment and those cheap items didn't make the move. They were falling apart, and the movers wouldn't touch one of them because it would have fallen over once it moved away from the wall.

When I moved into my second apartment, I invested in a quality piece of furniture: a ladder shelving unit. And after five moves, that piece of furniture is still in our house. Do not feel like you need to invest all your money in all the pieces right away. Go slow and find things that work for you.

Quality items can totally come from a thrift shop or repurpose store. We have a piece of furniture that has been handed down from my husband's grandparents, to his father, to us. We made the piece of furniture ours by painting it and changing the handles. Because the piece of furniture is well-built, we didn't have to worry about it falling apart. You can re-stain, paint, change the pulls—there are so many ways to bring old furniture to life and fit in your home without purchasing something new. Remember that when looking for quality.

More does not equal better. It is not worth your time, money, or energy to have tons of decor pieces all over your home. That is why I love shopping our home first. I don't have to spend any money. I don't have to go hunting for new things in a store. I can keep things simple and I can easily change out the look of a room.

Organize Like a Pro

When organizing your home, you also want to think about ways to decorate it. Use these tips to get your home looking how you want.

- Start buying decor pieces that can go together with items already in your home.
- Define your decorating style; use adjectives to give it more emotion.
- Only search for items that work with your adjectives.
- Declutter items that no longer work with your decorating style.
- Only buy quality items when you can (thrift store items included!).
- Don't buy into decorating fads.
- Include your family in the process.
- Always shop your home first, then find missing pieces second.
- Style things by using the rule of three.
- If it speaks to you, then it should be displayed somewhere in your home.

CHAPTER 20

Where to Go from Here

You have made a commitment to yourself, so do your best to show up and keep things organized. Put your new organizing habits to the test and see how they work for you and your family. Focus on what organizing means to you while enlisting your family's help. You can no longer call yourself disorganized or become overwhelmed by perfectionism because you have the tools and habits to stay focused.

Use the following checklist and worksheets to help you stay on track and create lasting order in your home. If you run out of space, use a separate piece of paper or your journal to answer the prompts on the worksheets. Enjoy the process and remember that slow and steady is how you can succeed in having an organized home. The worksheets are meant to be a guide to help you maintain order and figure out what order means to you; use them however feels the most helpful to you. Skip some, do them all, do them in order or don't— it's up to you!

Let's get organized and keep those habits going!

Organize Like a Pro

These are some simple habits to live by to keep yourself organized.

- Get rid of mental clutter.
- Write down your organizing habits.
- Write down changes you make to your old routines.
- Make checklists to keep you focused.
- Use a habit tracker.
- Enlist someone as an accountability partner.
- Reward yourself for changing your habits.
- Follow through with organizing habits.

Defining What "Organized" Means to You

Quickly scan the room you are in. Use the space below to write down any thoughts that pop into your head about the space. Everything and anything is welcome.

Your Organizing Habits Part 1

Use this page to go through every area of your home, looking at each space thoroughly. Open drawers and cabinets. Look at shelving, wall decor, paint color, and pillows. Focus on finding order in every nook and cranny, because you are organized. You just aren't giving yourself enough credit!

Space

What did you notice was organized?

What makes this space feel organized to you?

CHECKLIST

- ◯ Go through each room.
- ◯ Open drawers, cabinets, closets, and find order in every part of the space.
- ◯ Pick out at least one thing that feels organized.

Your Organizing Habits Part 2

1. What is the first thing you do after you get up and out of bed?

2. What do you do when you see an item that is on your counter but doesn't belong there?

3. What areas of your home do you clean up every night?

4. How quickly do you get rid of junk mail?

5. What do you do with your paper piles?

Creating New Organizational Habits

1. What are you or your family members unhappy about?

2. What habits can you tweak to work for everyone in the household?

3. What small things can you let go of?

CHECKLIST

As you create new habits, remember to:

○ Start small.

○ Figure out what is realistic for everyone.

○ Tweak habit as you go.

○ Create organizational systems that work for everyone, especially the most disorganized person in the house.

○ Delegate tasks.

4. What are your expectations for yourself and your family members?

Habit Changes

1. What habits have you tweaked?

2. What habits have not worked?

3. What organizational system has worked for your family?

Disorganized Family Member(s)

1. Write down what is bothering you about the "disorganized person's" habits.

2. Write down routines the "disorganized person" is already doing.

3. Brainstorm some ideas for tweaking that habit.

4. Pick one idea and test it out. After a few weeks, if it isn't working, pick a new idea to try.

Overcoming Perfectionist Tendencies

1. What do you want things to look like?

2. How do you want the space to be used?

3. How is the space being used now?

4. What is the feeling of your home?

5. What do you want your home to feel like?

Letting Go of Overwhelm

Here's a quick exercise to help you combat feeling overwhelmed around organizing.

1. Do a brain dump and write down every little project or task.

2. Take each task and break it down into smaller tasks. For example, I start with the least intimidating topic on my list. Let's say it's organizing the pantry. I walk into the pantry and look around. Then I write down all the steps I need to do to organize the space.

- Step one would be to take everything out of the pantry.
- Step two would be wiping all the shelves clean with cleaning supplies.
- Step three would be removing items that are expired.
- Step four would be grouping items together.
- And finally, the last step is to put everything back in the pantry.

3. Create a mini checklist here and use this to cross off each task.

○

○

○

○

○

○

Bedrooms Guide, Part 1

Is there a space in your bedroom that feels organized?

What organization system is working in your bedroom?

What organization system is not working in your bedroom?

What is your partner's organization system?

Desired habit changes for your bedroom:

Bedrooms Guide, Part 2

1. What is on the top of your desired habits list?

2. What can you remove from your bedroom that doesn't belong?

3. What clothes are you having trouble giving away? Why?

CHECKLIST

Remove any clothing that is:

- ◯ Ripped or stained
- ◯ Doesn't fit anymore
- ◯ Has not been worn for a long time
- ◯ You don't like

4. What are you willing to let go of from your closet?

The Kitchen, Part 1

1. How do you feel about your kitchen at this moment?

2. What are your current kitchen habits?

3. What is one thing that feels organized about your kitchen?

4. What are the kitchen habits you would like to change?

CHECKLIST

When organizing your kitchen, these steps will help keep you on track:

- ( ) Set a time when you will organize your kitchen.

- ( ) Decide whether you are labeling first or removing unused items first.

- ( ) Take action and declutter.

- ( ) Add sticky notes with each category on cabinets and shelves.

- ( ) Place items on shelves and in drawers without organizers.

- ( ) If you find items you don't use, remove them from your kitchen.

- ( ) Find organizing products that work for your drawer or cabinet.

- ( ) Store seasonal items together.

- ( ) Try storing holiday items with holiday decor.

- ( ) Remove the emotional attachment to sentimental kitchen items.

- ( ) Maintain your newly organized kitchen space by labeling everything.

- ( ) Get the family to help keep things tidy.

- ( ) Do a daily declutter of any drawer or cabinet you use by scanning the drawer and removing things that you don't need when you notice them.

WHERE TO GO FROM HERE

The Kitchen, Part 2

Take inventory of your kitchen items and write them down here.

1. What items do you use?

2. What items can you get rid of or don't need?

Shared Spaces

1. Do a walk-through of your space. What is working?

2. What is not working?

3. What organizational habits do you wish your family would take on?

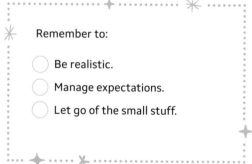

Remember to:

○ Be realistic.

○ Manage expectations.

○ Let go of the small stuff.

Define Each Room's Purpose

Room name:

Purpose for the room:

Room name:

Purpose for the room:

Room name:

Purpose for the room:

Room name:

Purpose for the room:

Room name:

Purpose for the room:

Room name:

Purpose for the room:

Office Guide

What do you want to use your office for?

List items that you need to keep in this space here.

List items that you know instantly you can get rid of here.

Use this space to create a visual of the room and create zones (see page 83).

Bathrooms Guide

1. What is the purpose of this bathroom?

2. Take inventory of the items in your bathroom and list them here.

3. Check the shelf life of the items in your bathroom and write down which items you can get rid of right away.

4. Write down the items you can move out of your bathroom (this can be items you are keeping or giving away).

5. List the items you use frequently here.

Kids' Rooms

1. What do you envision for your kids' rooms?

2. What does your child feel "organized" means to them?

3. How can you combine your vision with what you child feels is organized?

4. What habits will your child take on and be responsible for?

Kids' Habit Tracker

Create a mock habit tracker for your kids here to help you and your child figure out what's realistic. Write down the date and the day of the week and what habits you'd like them to take on.

Habit:

	M	T	W	T	F	SA	SU
	◯	◯	◯	◯	◯	◯	◯
	◯	◯	◯	◯	◯	◯	◯
	◯	◯	◯	◯	◯	◯	◯
	◯	◯	◯	◯	◯	◯	◯
	◯	◯	◯	◯	◯	◯	◯
	◯	◯	◯	◯	◯	◯	◯
	◯	◯	◯	◯	◯	◯	◯
	◯	◯	◯	◯	◯	◯	◯
	◯	◯	◯	◯	◯	◯	◯
	◯	◯	◯	◯	◯	◯	◯
	◯	◯	◯	◯	◯	◯	◯
	◯	◯	◯	◯	◯	◯	◯
	◯	◯	◯	◯	◯	◯	◯
	◯	◯	◯	◯	◯	◯	◯

Kids' Habit Tracker

Habit:

	M	T	W	T	F	SA	SU
....	◯	◯	◯	◯	◯	◯	◯
....	◯	◯	◯	◯	◯	◯	◯
....	◯	◯	◯	◯	◯	◯	◯
....	◯	◯	◯	◯	◯	◯	◯
....	◯	◯	◯	◯	◯	◯	◯
....	◯	◯	◯	◯	◯	◯	◯
....	◯	◯	◯	◯	◯	◯	◯
....	◯	◯	◯	◯	◯	◯	◯
....	◯	◯	◯	◯	◯	◯	◯
....	◯	◯	◯	◯	◯	◯	◯
....	◯	◯	◯	◯	◯	◯	◯
....	◯	◯	◯	◯	◯	◯	◯
....	◯	◯	◯	◯	◯	◯	◯
....	◯	◯	◯	◯	◯	◯	◯
....	◯	◯	◯	◯	◯	◯	◯

Minimizing Toys

1. What toys do your kids love to play with?

2. What toys can you get rid of?

3. What books are they reading now?

4. What does "done" look like? Describe it or draw it.

5. What steps do you need to take to get your room looking like it is done?

Paper Clutter

1. Will you need this paper again for legal purposes? These are for things like tax documents, mortgage or rental agreements, birth certificates, marriage licenses, contracts, etc.

2. Do you need the paper as a resource document? If you do, can you make it digital? Or can you find that same information online?

3. Is this piece of paper a certificate for something someone achieved? If so, why is it not on display?

4. Check the date. Is this document even relevant anymore? Sometimes we hold on to old papers that we no longer need, simply because they have a spot in our filing cabinet.

5. Can you get this digitally going forward? These are for things like bank statements, insurance documents, any form of bills, receipts, etc.

6. Is this a manual and can you get it online instead? I am not a fan of holding on to manuals for most things because we can usually find them online. Download the digital manual and save it to your computer. Then you still have the manual, just not the paper copy taking up space in your home.

WHERE TO GO FROM HERE

Habit Tracker

Use this worksheet to keep track of your habits.

Old habit:

New habit:

Thank You

Words cannot begin to express my gratitude to all who have made this book a possibility. Writing this book has been an absolute dream. It has been a goal of mine to be able to write a book about a topic I love. I am so proud that I believed in myself, that I put forth the effort to make this happen, and that I was able to chase my dream.

Thank you to my husband, Ben, for his continued support and encouragement. Your motivation and "pep talks" got me through some of those challenging days. You are right: "Litmans don't quit."

Thank you to my kids for "leaving me alone" to write, edit, and revise. And for giving me tons of inspiration that led to this book.

Thank you to my parents, Debbie and Jim, for always encouraging me to be the best version of myself.

Thank you to my brother, Tommy Bomberg, who always reminds me to manage my expectations.

Thank you to my in-laws, Jeff and Paula Litman for reading this book before your son. And, yes, I do write like that.

Thank you to my publisher, Rage Kindelsperger. Without you believing in my vision for this book, I don't think it would have turned out half as well as it did.

Thank you to my editor, Keyla Pizarro-Hernández, for turning my ramblings into functional sentences, and for keeping me focused on the task at hand.

Thank you to my incredible team, Kristin Kaplan, Latasha Doyle, Ally Carolan, Brittnay Deeds, and Reesa Myers, for keeping the rest of The Organized Mama running so smoothly while I focused on writing this book.

Thank you to Andrea Rappaport and Jessie Hearn for making me look and feel incredible. And for literally giving me the shirt off your back.

Thank you to Brian. Your memory has inspired me to do things I have always been scared to do. You are my reminder that life is short and to follow my dreams—no matter how scary they may be.

Thank you to Harry + Emma, and Karen Klein for allowing me to take pictures in your homes. I am so lucky to have friends like you!

And thank you to my clients for giving me the stories and pictures to share. I am so grateful for my friends and neighbors who had to listen to me talk about this book for what felt like ages, along with watching my kids while I was writing.

I am forever grateful for my incredible followers, subscribers, and social media friends. Supporting you on your organizing journey makes me excited to get up and work every single day!

References

Dauch, C., M. Imwalle, B. Ocasio, and A. E. Metz. (2018). "The Influence of the Number of Toys in the Environment on Toddlers' Play." *Infant Behavior and Development* 50: 78–87. https://www.sciencedirect.com/science/article/abs/pii/S0163638317301613.

Elkind, D. (2007). *The Power of Play: Learning What Comes Naturally.* Boston: Da Capo Press.

Gessert, L. (n.d.). "Is Paper Weighing You Down?" NAPO blog. https://blog.napo.net/blog/p4078.

Hirshkowitz, M., et al. (2015). "National Sleep Foundation's Sleep Time Duration Recommendations: Methodology and Results Summary." *Sleep Health* 1 (1): 40–43. https://pubmed.ncbi.nlm.nih.gov/29073412.

Jewell, S. (October 23, 2011). "The Nursery That Took All the Children's Toys Away." *The Independent.* https://www.independent.co.uk/news/education/education-news/the-nursery-that-took-all-the-children-s-toys-away-1125048.html.

Magnusson, M. (2019). *The Gentle Art of Swedish Death Cleaning.* New York: Simon & Schuster.

Montessori, M., A. E. George, and H. W. Holmes. (2015). *The Montessori Method: Scientific Pedagogy as Applied to Child Education in "the Children's Houses" with Additions and Revisions by the Author.* Andesite Press.

Payne, K. J., and L. M. Ross. (2010). *Simplicity Parenting: Using the Extraordinary Power of Less to Raise Calmer, Happier, and More Secure Kids.* New York: Ballantine Books.

Roster, C. A., J. R. Ferrari, and M. Peter Jurkat. (2016). "The Dark Side of Home: Assessing Possession 'Clutter' on Subjective Well-Being." *Journal of Environmental Psychology* 46: 32–41. https://doi.org/10.1016/j.jenvp.2016.03.003.

Ruder, D. B. (2019). "Screen Time and the Brain." Harvard Medical School, News & Research. https://hms.harvard.edu/news/screen-time-brain#:~:text=A%20good%20night's%20sleep%20is,secretion%20of%20the%20hormone%20melatonin.

Smith, M. (2019). *Cozy Minimalist Home: More Style, Less Stuff.* Grand Rapids, MI: Zondervan.

Thacher, P., and A. Reinheimer. (2018). "People at Risk of Hoarding Disorder May Have Serious Complaints About Sleep." American Academy of Sleep Medicine. https://aasm.org/people-at-risk-of-hoarding-disorder-may-have-serious-complaints-about-sleep.

Further Resources

Here are some other books that will help you in your organizing journey.

The Afrominimalist's Guide to Living with Less
by Christine Platt

Beautifully Organized
by Nikki Boyd

Cozy Minimalist Home
by Myquillyn Smith

The Gentle Art of Swedish Death Cleaning
by Margareta Magnusson

The Holistic Guide to Decluttering
by Michele Vig

The Lazy Genius Way
by Kendra Adachi

Outer Order, Inner Calm
by Gretchen Rubin

Simply Spaced
by Monica Leed

Take Back Your Time
by Morgan Tyree

About the Author

Former teacher turned professional organizer, **Jessica Litman**, also known as The Organized Mama, brings her teaching skills and passion for organizing to help families find the calm within their homes by clearing the clutter. She encourages families to embrace their homes while incorporating fun and easy home organizational habits that every family member can do. She has been recognized by People.com as an "organizing and DIY expert." Her industry-leading work has been featured in *Better Homes and Gardens, Parents Magazine,* and the *Boston Globe.* When Jessica isn't organizing, she can be found hanging out with her family, reading books, or tending to her garden. To connect, visit her website at https://www.theorganizedmama.com or her Instagram @organizedmamas.